SIMPLY NEW

THE WALK OF THE BELIEVER
HELP FOR YOUR NEW CHRISTIAN JOURNEY!

ELIZABETH JEAN

SIMPLY NEW
WALK OF THE BELIEVER
HELP FOR YOUR NEW CHRISTIAN JOURNEY!

Copyright © 2020 Elizabeth Jean
Cover Design: C Marcel Wiggins

Published by MIGMIR Company USA, LLC
All rights reserved. No part of this publication may be reproduced, distributed or transmitted in any form or by any means, without prior written permission. Unless otherwise identified, scripture quotations are from the King James Version of the Bible.

Rekindled Flame Publishing House
an imprint of

MIGMIR Company USA, LLC

www.migmir.us

For Worldwide Distribution
Printed in the U.S.A.

ISBN: 9781952253034

Library of Congress Control Number: 2020902726

TABLE OF CONTENTS

Acknowledgments 4

Introduction 5

Chapter One: Salvation 7

Chapter Two: Baptism in water 21

Chapter Three: Baptism in the Holy Spirit 29

Chapter Four: Words used in the church 35

Chapter Five: Our daily walk (Pt. One) 49

Chapter Six: Bible reading and study 53

Chapter Seven: Prayer 61

Chapter Eight: Church attendance 75

Chapter Nine: Giving 87

Chapter Ten: Healing 95

Chapter Eleven: Forgiveness 103

Chapter Twelve: Love 127

Chapter Thirteen: Our daily walk (Pt. Two) ... 143

My walk with God (Journal Section) 148

ACKNOWLEDGMENTS

I dedicate this book to my mother Leah Henderson, who as a teen was led to the Lord. After she was led to the Lord, they dropped her. There are many like her who have been abandoned by the Evangelists who led them to the Lord. I hope this book will help her and others to learn what to do.

Thank you, James Ryan, for the use of your computer and your encouragement to finish this book. It was by your help I finally got the work done.

Thank you, Pastor Paul Ortiz, for taking the time out of your busy schedule to read this material and critique it.

INTRODUCTION

We have accepted the Lord. We have been led in the sinner's prayer. What do we do next? Where do we go from here? Who is going to help us learn what we need to do next?

This book is designed for young believers to grow. It is designed to minister the basics of what is necessary to grow in the Lord. I hope to have defined some words used in the church and in the Bible. It concludes with forgiveness, love, and how to walk out the daily walk. We need to know these things.

Some areas we will cover are salvation, baptism in water, baptism in the Spirit, Bible reading, prayer, church attendance, giving healing, and our daily walk. These are areas that are important to the body of Christ. As we explore them, we will learn how to walk out our faith.

The Scriptures used come from the King James Version. The reader may compare the verses with other versions to see how accurate the study was. Also, you will find material from the Vine's Dictionary and Strong's Concordance.

CHAPTER ONE
SALVATION

What is salvation? It is not joining a church. It is not going to the front and getting on a church roll. It is not repeating a few words after someone. While these are nice, they don't save us. It is important to speak to God through Jesus, but it is important that it is done in faith.

Salvation is belief in Jesus and what He did on Calvary. Salvation, according to Vine's Dictionary means deliverance and preservation. In other words, it means deliverance from sin and preservation in the kingdom of God.

When we discuss salvation, we need to recognize some important facts. We need to recognize God is almighty; God created man; sin entered the world; Jesus died for our sins; confess our sins; and accept Jesus as Savior. As we cover these facts, we will see how God sets us free.

(1) God is Almighty and full of love.

We need to recognize God is Almighty. He is who He says He is. He sent His Son Jesus to earth to save anybody who wants to be saved. The Bible does not define who God is, but rather makes it clear He has always been and is always here.

Genesis 1:1: *In the beginning God created the heaven and the earth.*

John 1:1: *In the beginning was the Word, and the Word was with God, and the Word was God.*

John 1:14: *And the Word was made flesh, and dwelt among us (and we beheld his glory, the glory as of the only begotten of the Father,) full of grace and truth.*

Matthew 1:21: *And she shall bring forth a son and thou shalt call his name Jesus: for he shall save his people from his sins.*

CHAPTER ONE: SALVATION

In all these Scriptures, we understand that God and His Son have always been here. Jesus came to earth to show us who the Father is. He wants to show everyone that God is full of love.

John 3:16, 17: *For God so loved the world, that he gave his only begotten Son, that whosoever believeth in him should not perish, but have everlasting life. For God sent not his Son into the world to condemn the world; but that the world through him might be saved.*

God loves us enough to show us mercy through His Son. He did not want to condemn the world, but rather to save the world. Unfortunately, the world does not want to be saved. They would rather come up with another salvation, but that is for another time and another book. Suffice it to say, there is only one way to the Father. That way, is through Jesus Christ. We will explore this later in the chapter.

(2) God created man.

Genesis 1:26, 27: *And God said, Let us make man in our image, after our likeness: and let them have dominion over the fish of the sea, and over the fowl of the air, and over the cattle, and over all the earth, and over every* *creeping thing that creepeth upon the earth. So God created man in his own image, in the image of God created he him; male and female created he them.*

Psalms 139:13-16: *For thou hast possessed my reins; thou hast covered me in my mother's womb. I will praise thee, for I am fearfully and wonderfully made: marvelous are thy works, and that my soul knoweth right well. My substance was not hid from thee, when I was made in secret, and curiously wrought in the lowest parts of the earth. Thine eyes did see my substance, yet being imperfect; and in thy book all my members were written, which is in continuance were fashioned, when as yet there was none of them.*

Notice in these verses, we were created in the image of God. We are not products of evolution. We are not descendants of monkeys. The Scripture is very clear. The reason people deny this truth, is they do not think they need a savior. They are very wrong.

Another issue we need to address is God did not create two males or two females. He created male and female. He intended to fill the earth with people. Two of the same sex would not be able to fill the earth. It takes opposite sexes to do this. God did not create homosexuals and lesbians. The way we are

CHAPTER ONE: SALVATION

is a matter of choice because of problems in the past. We need to go to God for help and stay close to Him for complete deliverance.

(3) Sin entered the world.

Genesis 2:15-17: *The Lord God took the man and put him into the garden of Eden to dress it and to keep it. And the Lord God commanded man, saying, Of every tree of the garden thou mayest freely eat: but the tree of the knowledge of good and evil, thou shalt not eat of it: for in the day that thou eatest thereof thou shalt surely die.*

Genesis 2:25: *And they were both naked, the man and his wife and were not ashamed.*

Genesis 3:1-21: *Now the serpent was more subtil than any beast of the field which the Lord God had made. And he said unto the woman, Yea, hath God said, Ye shall not eat of every tree of the garden? And the woman said unto the serpent, We may eat of the fruit of the trees of the garden: But of the fruit of the tree which is in the midst of the garden, God hath said, Ye shall not eat of it, neither shall ye touch it, lest ye die. And the serpent said unto the woman, Ye shall not surely die: For God doth know that in the day ye eat thereof, then your eyes shall be opened, and ye shall be as gods, knowing good and evil. And when the woman saw that the tree was good for food, and that it was pleasant* *to the eyes, and a tree to be desired to make one wise, she took of the fruit thereof, and did eat, and gave also unto her husband with her; and he did eat. And the eyes of them both were opened, and they knew that they were naked; and they sewed fig leaves together, and made themselves aprons. And they heard the voice of the Lord God walking in the garden in the cool of the day: and Adam and his wife hid themselves from the presence of the Lord God amongst the trees of the garden. And the Lord God called unto Adam, and said unto him, Where art thou? And he said, I heard thy voice in the garden, and I was afraid, because I was naked; and I hid myself. And he said, Who told thee that thou wast naked? Hast thou eaten of the tree, whereof I commanded thee that thou shouldest not eat? And the man said, The woman whom thou gavest to be with me, she gave me of the tree, and I did eat. And the Lord God said unto the woman, What is this that thou hast done? And the woman said, The serpent beguiled me, and I did eat. And the Lord God said unto the serpent, Because thou hast done this, thou art cursed above all cattle, and above every beast of the field; upon thy belly shalt thou go, and dust shalt thou eat all the days of thy life: And I will put enmity between thee and the woman, and between thy seed and her seed; it shall bruise thy head, and thou shalt bruise his heel. Unto the woman he said, I will greatly multiply thy sorrow and thy conception; in sorrow thou*

CHAPTER ONE: SALVATION

shalt bring forth children; and thy desire shall be to thy husband, and he shall rule over thee. And unto Adam he said, Because thou hast hearkened unto the voice of thy wife, and hast eaten of the tree, of which I commanded thee, saying, Thou shalt not eat of it: cursed is the ground for thy sake; in sorrow shalt thou eat of it all the days of thy life; Thorns also and thistles shall it bring forth to thee; and thou shalt eat the herb of the field; In the sweat of thy face shalt thou eat bread, till thou return unto the ground; for out of it wast thou taken: for dust thou art, and unto dust shalt thou return. And Adam called his wife's name Eve; because she was the mother of all living. Unto Adam also and to his wife did the Lord God make coats of skins, and clothed them.

When the man and woman disobeyed God, they died spiritually. They were separated from God. We were separated from God because of what was done. Let us look at a few things. God gave a simple command. The man and woman chose to disobey that command. Instead of admitting they were guilty, they blamed one another. If they had admitted their sin, they would have been forgiven. Instead, they were cursed. God did offer the first blood sacrifice when He made coats from animals. When we admit we are sinners, we will be forgiven. Jesus became the sin offering for us.

Romans 3:23: *For all have sinned, and come short of the glory of God:*

Romans 6:23: *For the wages of sin is death; but the gift of God is eternal life through Jesus Christ our Lord.*

We need to come to the place where we admit we are sinners. We need to realize that as sinners, we deserve death. We are separated from God because of that sin. It is not necessarily anything specific we have done. It is our very sin nature that condemns us.

Once we recognize that, we will have a chance to be forgiven and saved. We can have a new life.

(4) Jesus came!

Jesus came, died, and rose again to deal with the sin nature. He came to earth as a baby, lived a sinless life on earth, died, rose again, and returned to Heaven. He did what was necessary to atone for our sin. He suffered for us so we can be free. There are many Scriptures that attest to that fact. We need to realize Jesus did what was necessary.

Philippians 2:5-9: *Let this mind be in you,*

CHAPTER ONE: SALVATION

which was also in Christ Jesus: who being in the form of God, thought it not robbery to be equal with God: but made himself of no reputation, and took upon him the form of a servant, and was made in the likeness of men: and being found in fashion as a man, he humbled himself, and became obedient unto death, even the death of the cross. Wherefore God also hath highly exalted him, and given him a name which is above every name...

Matthew 4:1-11: *Then was Jesus led up of the Spirit into the wilderness to be tempted of the devil. And when he had fasted forty days and forty nights, he was afterward an hungred. And when the tempter came to him, he said, If thou be the Son of God, command that these stones be made bread. But he answered and said, It is written, Man shall not live by bread alone, but by every word that proceedeth out of the mouth of God. Then the devil taketh him up into the holy city, and setteth him on a pinnacle of the temple, And saith unto him, If thou be the Son of God, cast thyself down: for it is written, He shall give his angels charge concerning thee: and in their hands they shall bear thee up, lest at any time thou dash thy foot against a stone. Jesus said unto him, It is written again, Thou shalt not tempt the Lord thy God. Again, the devil taketh him up into an exceeding high mountain, and sheweth him all the kingdoms of the world, and the glory of them; And saith* *unto him, All these things will I give thee, if thou wilt fall down and worship me. Then saith Jesus unto him, Get thee hence, Satan: for it is written, Thou shalt worship the Lord thy God, and him only shalt thou serve. Then the devil leaveth him, and, behold, angels came and ministered unto him.*

<u>1 Corinthians 1:17, 18:</u> *For Christ sent me not to baptize, but to preach the gospel: not with wisdom of words, lest the cross of Christ should be made of none effect. For the preaching of the cross is to them that perish foolishness; but unto us which are saved it is the power of God.*

Jesus was willing to humble Himself as a man so He could go through everything we have gone through, but without sin. After the Holy Spirit had filled Jesus, He led Him into the wilderness. Jesus faced the same temptations Adam and Eve faced, but without sin. He quoted the Word to fend off the devil. He left us an example to follow. We preach the cross to those around us to show what Jesus did. We can tell everyone the good news of what Jesus did for us.

CHAPTER ONE: SALVATION

(5) Confess our sins.

Once we accept what Jesus did for us, we need to admit we are sinners. Because we have admitted we are sinners and Jesus died for our sin, we need to be forgiven. Jesus gave us new life.

Ephesians 1:7: *In whom we have redemption through his blood, the forgiveness of sins, according to the riches of his grace*

Colossians 2:14: *Blotting out the handwriting of ordinances that was against us, which was contrary to us, and took it out of the way, nailing it to his cross;*

1 John 1:9: *If we confess our sins, he is faithful and just to forgive us our sins, and to cleanse us from all unrighteousness.*

It is through the work of Jesus we are forgiven. Because we follow through with this knowledge, we will come to a new understanding of what we have to do to become believers. While the above Scripture in 1 John is written to believers, unbelievers can appropriate the verse to admit they are sinners and receive forgiveness.

(6) Accept Jesus.

We need to accept Jesus as Savior, accept His forgiveness, and confess Jesus as Savior.

Romans 10:9, 10: *That if thou shalt confess with thy mouth the Lord Jesus, and shalt believe in thine heart that God hath raised him from the dead, thou shalt be saved. For with the heart man believeth unto righteousness, and with the mouth confession is made unto salvation.*

When we speak the Word of God in our lives, we will be saved. We need to confess what Jesus did for us. Now that we have seen what the Gospel says, we need to take the next step. While the words are not important, we do offer a simple prayer to those who would accept Jesus.

Dear Jesus, I admit I am a sinner. I ask You to forgive my sins. I accept You as my Lord and Savior. Take my life and do with it as You will. Thank you for saving me. I pray this in Jesus name, amen.

When we speak the Word of God in our lives, we will be saved.

Once we ask Jesus into our hearts and believe it, we need to realize the enemy is going to fight us. We

CHAPTER ONE: SALVATION

will hear whispers saying, "Did we really get saved"? "It was all emotion". There are other lies that can be mentioned, but they are not important. As we realize they are lies, we can rejoice in the fact that Jesus, through the Holy Spirit, has done the work.

In addition, we need to tell others of what we have done. As our lives change, we will be witnesses of what Jesus has done. We will see great growth!

SIMPLY NEW: WALK OF THE BELIEVER

AMAZING GRACE

Amazing grace! how sweet the sound,
That saved a wretch; like me!
once was lost, but now am found,
Was blind, but now I see.

'Twas grace that taught my heart to fear,
And grace my fears relieved;
How precious did that grace appear
The hour I first believed!

The Lord hath promised good to me,
His word my hope secures;
He will my shield and portion be
As long as life endures.

When we've been there ten thousand years,
Bright shining as the sun,
We've no less days to sing God's praise
Than when we first begun.

CHAPTER TWO
BAPTISM IN WATER

After salvation, we want to show the whole world what we have done inwardly. We want to get baptized. What is baptism? According to Vine's Dictionary, it is the processes of immersion, submersion, and emergence. It is not sprinkling with water. It is not infant baptism. It is for people who reach the age of accountability. They know and understand the difference between right and wrong. They recognize their need for a Savior and want to renounce sin. Baptism is the public action that demonstrates what was done on the inside in the Spirit.

Acts 2:37, 38: *Now when they heard this, they were pricked in their heart, and said unto Peter and to the rest of the Apostles, Men and brethren what shall we do? Then Peter said unto them, Repent, and be baptized every one of you in the name of Jesus Christ for the remission of sins, and ye shall receive the gift of the Holy Ghost.*

This passage makes clear what we are supposed to do and the order in which we are to do it. As we do this, we will receive all of what the Lord has for us.

Matthew 28:18-20: *And Jesus came and spake unto them, saying, All power is given unto me in heaven and in earth. Go ye therefore, and teach all nations, baptizing them in the name of the Father, and of the Son, and of the Holy Ghost: Teaching them to observe all things whatsoever I have commanded you: and, lo, I am with you always, even unto the end of the world. Amen.*

Mark 16:15, 16: *And he said unto them, Go ye into all the world, and preach the gospel to every creature. He that believeth and is baptized shall be saved; but he that believeth*

CHAPTER TWO: BAPTISM IN WATER

not shall be damned.

These passages make it very clear that Jesus wants us to baptize those we bring to Him. We have the assurance that He is always with us, no matter what. We have nothing to be afraid of. Baptism is a requirement, not an option.

Romans 6:3-6: *Know ye not, that so many of us as were baptized into Jesus Christ were baptized into his death? Therefore we are buried with him by baptism into death: that like as Christ was raised up from the dead by the glory of the Father, even so we also should walk in newness of life. For if we have been planted together in the likeness of his death, we shall be also in the likeness of his resurrection: Knowing this, that our old man is crucified with him, that the body of sin might be destroyed, that henceforth we should not serve sin.*

Colossians 2:12: *Buried with him in baptism, wherein also ye are risen with him through the faith of the operation of God, who hath raised him from the dead.*

In these passages, we see what Jesus did on Calvary, in the grave, and in rising again. In baptism, we realize we are dead to sin and alive to Christ. We need to realize this is all symbolic. This action comes as a result of what we did at salvation.

Now I want to deal with a controversial issue: infant baptism. Infant baptism is not scriptural. It was invented to make parents feel good. As we have seen, baptism is total immersion in water. Babies can't be baptized that way. Besides, they have no concept of what's happening—let alone to agree with it.

Matthew 19:13-15: *Then were there brought unto him little children, that he should put his hands on them, and pray: and the disciples rebuked them. But Jesus said, Suffer little children, and forbid them not, to come unto me: for of such is the kingdom of heaven. And he laid his hands on them, and departed thence.*

Mark 10:13-16: *And they brought young children to him, that he should touch them: and his disciples rebuked those that brought them. But when Jesus saw it, he was much displeased, and said unto them, Suffer the little children to come unto me, and forbid them not: for of such is the kingdom of God. Verily I say unto you, Whosoever shall not receive the kingdom of God as a little child, he shall not enter therein. And he took them up in his arms, put his hands upon them, and blessed them.*

Luke 18:15-17: *And they brought unto him*

CHAPTER TWO: BAPTISM IN WATER

also infants, that he would touch them: but when his disciples saw it, they rebuked them. But Jesus called them unto him, and said, Suffer little children to come unto me, and forbid them not: for of such is the kingdom of God. Verily I say unto you, Whosoever shall not receive the kingdom of God as a little child shall in no wise enter therein.

We can see in these passages, parents brought the children to Jesus. Even though the parents were rebuked by the disciples, Jesus overrode the disciples and called the parents to Himself and blessed the children. Jesus emphasized the Kingdom of Heaven was for the children and young at heart. He said if we don't come as little children, we will never enter the Kingdom of Heaven. I'm not saying don't bring infants and little children to Jesus. That would be unscriptural. I am saying, we can dedicate them to Jesus and raise them in the nurture and admonition of the Lord.

Deuteronomy 6:7: *And thou shalt teach them diligently unto thy children, and shall talk of them when thou sittest in thine house, and when thou walkest by the way, and when thou liest down, and when thou risest up.*

Ephesians 6:4: *And ye fathers, provoke not your children to wrath: but bring them up in* *the nurture and admonition of the Lord.*

    These passages make it clear. We are to bring children to Jesus—we are to teach them about Him daily in everything we do. This does not mean we simply send them to Sunday School and church for them to do the teaching for us. It means we must take an interest in teaching them daily ourselves. It is not the church's responsibility to do all the teaching. They can help and reinforce what we are teaching them, but they are not a substitute.

    While infant baptism is wrong, because it is unscriptural, baby dedications are alright because Scripture is clear we are to bring our children to Jesus.

    Sprinkling is another issue I want to deal with. Nowhere in the Bible is "sprinkling" mentioned. Everywhere baptism is mentioned, immersion is clearly indicated. Even the thief was immersed in the rain when He accepted Jesus.

    As we can see, baptism is very important. Jesus commanded us to do it. The apostles described it. Paul did it on occasion—he was careful to avoid confusion and division in the church. We need to be careful that when we baptize, we recognize that Jesus is the source—not man. We only have to do it once because we are publicly proclaiming what Jesus did for us. To do

CHAPTER TWO: BAPTISM IN WATER

it more often belittles what Jesus did and contributes to division.

SIMPLY NEW: WALK OF THE BELIEVER

CHAPTER THREE
BAPTISM IN THE HOLY SPIRIT

Once we are saved and baptized in water, we are ready for the baptism in the Holy Spirit. This is just as important as the first two. I believe we can not have as full of a Christian life without it. I am not saying we don't receive the Holy Spirit at salvation; we do.

John 20:19-23: *Then the same day at evening, being the first day of the week, when the doors were shut where the disciples were assembled for fear of the Jews, came Jesus* *and stood in the midst, and saith unto them, Peace be unto you. And when he had so said, he shewed unto them his hands and his side. Then were the disciples glad, when they saw the Lord. Then said Jesus to them again, Peace be unto you: as my Father hath sent me, even so send I you. And when he had said this, he breathed on them, and saith unto them, Receive ye the Holy Ghost: Whose soever sins ye remit, they are remitted unto them; and whose soever sins ye retain, they are retained.*

Acts 2:1-4: *And when the day of Pentecost was fully come, they were all with one accord in one place. And suddenly there came a sound from heaven as of a rushing mighty wind, and it filled all the house where they were sitting. And there appeared unto them cloven tongues like as of fire, and it sat upon each of them. And they were all filled with the Holy Ghost, and began to speak with other tongues, as the Spirit gave them utterance.*

    These two passages make it clear there are two times we receive the Holy Spirit. The Holy Spirit woos us to our Lord in salvation. Then, He becomes resident in us. When we are filled with the Holy Spirit, we put Him in charge as our President, King, and Lord of our lives.

    The Scripture is very clear. We don't just

CHAPTER THREE: BAPTISM IN THE HOLY SPIRIT

"find Jesus as Lord." Without the Holy Spirit drawing us, we are not ready to receive.

John 3:1-8: *There was a man of the Pharisees, named Nicodemus, a ruler of the Jews: The same came to Jesus by night, and said unto him, Rabbi, we know that thou art a teacher come from God: for no man can do these miracles that thou doest, except God be with him. Jesus answered and said unto him, Verily, verily, I say unto thee, Except a man be born again, he cannot see the kingdom of God. Nicodemus saith unto him, How can a man be born when he is old? can he enter the second time into his mother's womb, and be born? Jesus answered, Verily, verily, I say unto thee, Except a man be born of water and of the Spirit, he cannot enter into the kingdom of God. That which is born of the flesh is flesh; and that which is born of the Spirit is spirit. Marvel not that I said unto thee, Ye must be born again. The wind bloweth where it listeth, and thou hearest the sound thereof, but canst not tell whence it cometh, and whither it goeth: so is every one that is born of the Spirit.*

John 14:15-18: *If ye love me, keep my commandments. And I will pray the Father, and he shall give you another Comforter, that he may abide with you for ever; Even the Spirit of truth; whom the world cannot receive, because it seeth him not, neither* *knoweth him: but ye know him; for he dwelleth with you, and shall be in you. I will not leave you comfortless: I will come to you.*

John 16:7-15: *Nevertheless I tell you the truth; It is expedient for you that I go away: for if I go not away, the Comforter will not come unto you; but if I depart, I will send him unto you. And when he is come, he will reprove the world of sin, and of righteousness, and of judgment: Of sin, because they believe not on me; Of righteousness, because I go to my Father, and ye see me no more; Of judgment, because the prince of this world is judged. I have yet many things to say unto you, but ye cannot bear them now. Howbeit when he, the Spirit of truth, is come, he will guide you into all truth: for he shall not speak of himself; but whatsoever he shall hear, that shall he speak: and he will shew you things to come. He shall glorify me: for he shall receive of mine, and shall shew it unto you. All things that the Father hath are mine: therefore said I, that he shall take of mine, and shall shew it unto you.*

    In these passages, we see Jesus gave the Holy Spirit to help us find our way to Him. It is by the Holy Spirit that we begin and continue our walk in Jesus daily.

CHAPTER THREE: BAPTISM IN THE HOLY SPIRIT

Since we already have this salvation, we need to move on to the baptism in the Holy Spirit. It is through this baptism that we receive power to minister to others. We also receive power to change our lives daily.

How do we know we are filled with the Holy Spirit? According to Acts 2:4, we will speak with other tongues as the Spirit gives us utterance.

What do we do with those who seek, but never speak in tongues? Do we tell them to keep seeking? Do we acknowledge the change in their lives?

I believe we should do both. We have to obey Scripture. If the change is evident in our lives, we acknowledge that. We go from darkness to light. The Holy Spirit will guide us to make changes necessary for growth and maturity.

Let us pray. Holy Spirit come into my life. I want You to take charge of my life. Show evidence of the infilling through speaking in tongues. I thank You for answering my prayer. I pray this in Jesus name. Amen.

SIMPLY NEW: WALK OF THE BELIEVER

CHAPTER FOUR
WORDS USED IN THE CHURCH

Many times we use words like regeneration, justification, sanctification, righteousness, and grace. What do these words mean? They are fancy words used to describe the walk of the believer. In this chapter we will discuss each word so we have a better understanding of them. We will look at Scripture to see how the Lord wants us to look at these words and how to apply them.

Regeneration

In regeneration, we see what happens at salvation. When we are born again, our sin nature dies. We become new creatures in Jesus Christ.

2 Corinthians 5:17: *Therefore if any man be in Christ, he is a new creature; old things are passed away, behold all things are become new.*

Isaiah 43:18, 19: *Remember ye not the former things, neither consider the things of old. Behold, I will do a new thing; now it shall spring forth; shall ye not know it? I will even make a way in the wilderness, and rivers in the desert.*

We know God promised to make all things new. We no longer have to walk in the ways of the world. The past is over. The future is bright. We need to put off the "old man" and put on the "new man."

Ephesians 2:14-17: *For he is our peace, who hath made both one, and hath broken down the middle wall of partition between us; Having abolished in his flesh the enmity, even the law of commandments contained in ordinances; for to make in himself of twain*

CHAPTER FOUR: WORDS USED IN THE CHURCH

one new man, so making peace; And that he might reconcile both unto God in one body by the cross, having slain the enmity thereby: And came and preached peace to you which were afar off, and to them that were nigh.

Ephesians 4:21-24: *If so be that ye have heard him, and have been taught by him, as the truth is in Jesus: That ye put off concerning the former conversation the old man, which is corrupt according to the deceitful lusts; And be renewed in the spirit of your mind; And that ye put on the new man, which after God is created in righteousness and true holiness.*

Colossians 3:10: *And have put on the new man which is renewed in knowledge after the image of him that created him.*

Regeneration is important. While it is mentioned twice specifically, the thought is all throughout the New Testament. Regeneration, according to Vine's Dictionary, means new birth, involving the communication of a new life, the two operating powers to produce which are the word of truth, and the Holy Spirit. According to Strong's Concordance, it means (spiritual) rebirth (the state or

When we put on the new man, we find a new freedom to be all that the Lord wants us to be.

act) that is spiritual renovation. It is the act of rebirth.

Matthew 19:28: *And Jesus said unto them, Verily I say unto you, That ye which have followed me, in the regeneration when the Son of man shall sit in the throne of his glory, ye also shall sit upon twelve thrones, judging the twelve tribes of Israel.*

Titus 3:5: *Not by works of righteousness which we have done, but according to his mercy he saved us, by the washing of regeneration, and the renewing of the Holy Ghost.*

Justification

Justification, according to Vine's Dictionary, primarily is to deem to be right, to show to be right or righteous. Strong's Concordance defines justification as acquittal (for Christ's sake) or an equitable deed by implication; a statute or decision. Another definition to the word is "just as if I had never sinned."

Romans 4:2: *For if Abraham were justified by works, he hath whereof to glory; but not before God.*

Romans 5:14-18: *Nevertheless death reigned*

CHAPTER FOUR: WORDS USED IN THE CHURCH

from Adam to Moses, even over them that had not sinned after the similitude of Adam's transgression, who is the figure of him that was to come. Not as the offence, so also is the free gift. For if through the offence of one many be dead, much more the grace of God, and the gift by grace, which is by one man, Jesus Christ, hath abounded unto many. And not as it was by one that sinned, so is the gift: for the judgment was by one to condemnation, but the free gift is of many offences unto justification. For if by one man's offence death reigned by one; much more they which receive abundance of grace and of the gift of righteousness shall reign in life by one, Jesus Christ.) Therefore as by the offence of one judgment came upon all men to condemnation; even so by the righteousness of one the free gift came upon all men unto justification of life.

    We cannot be saved by doing good works. It is done through the atoning work of the cross when Jesus died and shed His blood. Justification brings out the knowledge that we can't get to Heaven by our good works, but rather by grace (unmerited favor).

    Justification keeps us going on the right path to reach others for Christ. Like the rebirth and regeneration, justification is a once in a lifetime event. It comes as a result of what Jesus did on the cross. As we recognize our acquittal from our sin, we have a new sense of freedom. We are satisfied with life because we have Jesus as our High Priest Who intercedes for us.

Sanctification

While rebirth, regeneration, and justification are onetime events, sanctification is an ongoing process that develops us spiritually.

1 Corinthians 1:27-30: *But God hath chosen the foolish things of the world to confound the wise; and God hath chosen the weak things of the world to confound the things which are mighty; and base things of the world, and things which are despised hath God chosen, yea, and things which are not, to bring to nought things that are: that no flesh should glory in his presence. But of him are ye in Christ Jesus, who of God is made unto us wisdom, and righteousness, and sanctification, and redemption.*

2 Thessalonians: 2:13, 14: *But we are bound to give thanks always to God for you brethren beloved of the Lord, because God hath from the beginning chosen you to salvation through sanctification of the Spirit and belief of the truth: Whereunto he called you by our gospel, to the obtaining of the glory of our Lord Jesus*

CHAPTER FOUR: WORDS USED IN THE CHURCH

Christ.

In these verses, sanctification, according to Strong's Concordance, means purifier or holiness. According to Vine's Dictionary, sanctification is used of separation to God and the separation of the believer from evil things and ways.

We are purified and set apart for the Lord's use. We no longer desire the things we once did. As we look to the finished work of Calvary, we will not want to do anything to displease Him. We need to recognize it is not done all in one shot (not that it can't be), but rather as a day by day process that continuously removes everything in our lives that is not pleasing to the Lord. It can be a painful process as the Lord probes our motives, thoughts, memories, as well as our actions. Many, if not all, wrong behaviors fall away as we spend more time with the Lord developing a relationship with Him on a daily basis. As the Lord deals with our inner man, we find more freedom in our walk to become bolder.

We need to realize sanctification is not following a set of legalistic rules to please mankind. Rather it is grace to do right. It is a want to do right that brings about a sense of peace. While certain activities such as Bible reading, prayer, going to church, giving tithes and offerings, fasting, etc. help us in our daily walk, we must never make rituals and laws of them. Rather, we can use them as ways to develop a deeper relationship with our Father, in the Son, through the Holy Spirit. As we do this, we find we have no reason to fear, but rather can be bold. We will discover a new sense of freedom and peace as we no longer deal with habits or ways of dealing with things. We recognize we are covered by the blood of Jesus. We no longer desire things of the world.

Righteousness

The next term we want to cover is righteousness. Essentially, it means being in right standing with God. Vine's Dictionary defines righteousness as the character or quality of being right or just. It means that once we are saved, we become righteous. We walk out righteousness daily.

Romans 5:18-21: *Therefore as by the offence of one judgment came upon all men to condemnation; even so by the righteousness of one the free gift came upon all men unto justification of life. For as by one man's disobedience many were made sinners, so by the obedience of one shall many be made righteous. Moreover the law entered, that the offence might abound. But where sin*

CHAPTER FOUR: WORDS USED IN THE CHURCH

abounded, grace did much more abound: That as sin hath reigned unto death, even so might grace reign through righteousness unto eternal life by Jesus Christ our Lord.

2 Corinthians 5:20, 21: *Now then we are ambassadors for Christ, as though God did beseech you by us: we pray you in Christ's stead, be ye reconciled to God. For he hath made him to be sin for us, who knew no sin; that we might be made the righteousness of God in him.*

1 Peter 2:21-24: *For even hereunto were ye called: because Christ also suffered for us, leaving us an example, that ye should follow his steps: Who did no sin, neither was guile found in his mouth: Who, when he was reviled, reviled not again; when he suffered, he threatened not; but committed himself to him that judgeth righteously: Who his own self bare our sins in his own body on the tree, that we, being dead to sins, should live unto righteousness: by whose stripes ye were healed.*

In these three passages, we see this fact: When we have accepted Jesus as Lord and Savior, we became righteous. It is not something we earn, but it's placed on us. We can't earn this by doing good deeds, but rather receive it by faith. We need to accept this fact.

Isaiah 64:6: *But we are all as an unclean thing, and all our righteousnesses are as filthy rags; and we all do fade as a leaf; and our iniquities, like the wind, have taken us away.*

Romans 10:3: *For they being ignorant of God's righteousness, and going about to establish their own righteousness, have not submitted themselves unto the righteousness of God.*

What we do outside of salvation in Jesus is totally worthless. In the first Scripture above, the filthy rags are menstrual cloths. He compares our self-righteousness to the pads women wear at the time of their period. We know how nasty that is. We need to submit to God, and obey Him to become clean and righteous.

Now that is not to say we don't have to do anything in our Christian walk. Rather, we are to work in the things of the Lord. We are commanded to win souls.

Matthew 28:18-20: *And Jesus came and spake unto them, saying, All power is given unto me in heaven and in earth. Go ye therefore, and teach all nations, baptizing them in the name of the Father, and of the Son, and of the Holy Ghost: Teaching them to observe all things whatsoever I have*

CHAPTER FOUR: WORDS USED IN THE CHURCH

commanded you: and, lo, I am with you always, even unto the end of the world. Amen.

Mark 16:15-18: *And he said unto them, Go ye into all the world, and preach the gospel to every creature. He that believeth and is baptized shall be saved; but he that believeth not shall be damned. And these signs shall follow them that believe; In my name shall they cast out devils; they shall speak with new tongues; They shall take up serpents; and if they drink any deadly thing, it shall not hurt them; they shall lay hands on the sick, and they shall recover.*

Acts 1:4, 5, 8: *And, being assembled together with them, commanded them that they should not depart from Jerusalem, but wait for the promise of the Father, which, saith he, ye have heard of me. For John truly baptized with water; but ye shall be baptized with the Holy Ghost not many days hence. But ye shall receive power, after that the Holy Ghost is come upon you: and ye shall be witnesses unto me both in Jerusalem, and in all Judaea, and in Samaria, and unto the uttermost part of the earth.*

    We receive the Holy Spirit to minister to the lost. We can help others through the laying on of hands and removal of the enemy's imps. A note should be made as to Mark 16:18. When it talks of serpents and deadly drinks, it is not encouraging such behavior. Rather, if such actions happen by accident, the believer is protected. To do them on purpose is to put God to a foolish test. There is no guarantee of protection.

2 Timothy 2:15: *Study to shew thyself approved unto God, a workman that needeth not to be ashamed, rightly dividing the word of truth.*

Psalms 119:11: *Thy word have I hid in mine heart, that I might not sin against thee.*

    These two verses, (and other verses like them) instruct us to spend time in the Word that we may grow in the Lord. Our righteousness is developed through our time of studying the Word.

    Some of the things we can do is pray, give tithes, and other good works. As we do them through the leading of the Holy Spirit, our righteousness gets stronger. We need to remember righteousness is imputed or given to us, not earned. It is through our faith in Jesus, we are made righteous. We become stronger in our walk with Him as we do the things expected of us.

CHAPTER FOUR: WORDS USED IN THE CHURCH

Grace

The last term used by the church that should also be mentioned is grace. Grace is God's unmerited favor. Vine's Dictionary defines grace as: objective, that which bestows pleasure, delight, or causes favorable regard. Subjective, (1) on the part of the bestower, the friendly disposition from which the kindly proceeds... (2) on the part of the bestowed, a feeling of gratitude. This definition indicates God provides mercy and a refusal of judgment for our sins. Rather, he forgives them and puts us on the right path to walk out our salvation. On our part, we are grateful that the Lord does not hold our past against us. Rather He makes us new creatures in him.

Ephesians 2:4, 5, 8-10: *But God, who is rich in mercy, for his great love wherewith he loved us, Even when we were dead in sins, hath quickened us together with Christ, (by grace ye are saved;)... For by grace are ye saved through faith; and that not of yourselves: it is the gift of God: Not of works, lest any man should boast. For we are his workmanship, created in Christ Jesus unto good works, which God hath before ordained that we should walk in them.*

SIMPLY NEW: WALK OF THE BELIEVER

I believe what was done on Calvary opened the door for God to receive us as His own. Through the work of Jesus Christ we receive grace. Grace comes from the favor of God extending down to us. We don't have to earn grace. It is a free gift. If we had to work for it, then we would have to keep following rules and regulations to be saved. We know from the children of Israel that rules and regulations only bring condemnation, not love. God loves us too much to put us through that. To require works negates John 3:16. It also negates all the Scriptures listed on grace. We need to allow God to be God and give us His favor as we walk with Him.

    These words describe our Christian walk. We need to realize that each part is important to the work of Christ. Upon the new birth, we are regenerated and justified as we walk in the righteousness of the Lord. As we walk out our sanctification, we will be blessed. We need to recognize the grace we receive is not based on works, but on the finished work of Christ. We simply have to be obedient to the Lord so we will grow daily.

CHAPTER FIVE
OUR DAILY WALK PT. ONE

Once we have received the Lord in our hearts, have been baptized in water and in the Holy Ghost, we have to walk out our walk, pleasing to the Lord. So often, we are expected to know what to do as young believers. However, we usually don't. In the next few chapters, we will look at things that can be done to help us grow and mature.

There is nothing worse than a believer who does not mature. We are not to be spiritually retarded in our Christian life. We are to grow up and fulfill the plan of God in our daily lives. We will deal with this issue in another book. Suffice it to say, we should desire to grow and mature daily.

First, we are going to deal with reading the Bible on a daily basis. We need to get into the Scripture regularly to feed our spirit and to find out what God is saying to us. As we do, we will get stronger in our faith.

Second, we will deal with prayer. Prayer is a conversation with God. It consists of talking and listening. After we spend time reading the Bible, we need to ask the Lord how to apply what we have read, and how to live out our daily lives. There are times when we have a need to talk to the Father about specific problems and receive answers.

Third, we will deal with church attendance. As we spend time with the Lord in His Word and prayer, we should desire to get to know others of like precious faith. We want to hear what others say about the Scriptures we have read and the answers we have received.

Fourth, we will deal with giving. It is important to the work of God that we give to Him regularly. He has provided us a place to give that is safe. It is through our support that the church can reach others for the Lord.

Fifth, we will deal with spiritual and physical healing. We can't truly serve the

CHAPTER FIVE: OUR DAILY WALK PT. ONE

Lord with health problems. We can pray, but we can't truly witness as effectively as when we are well. I have some personal opinions on this matter, but we will look at the Scriptures first.

Sixth, we will deal with forgiveness. It is through forgiveness we see much healing. As we let go of hurts and pain, we no longer carry grudges or bitterness. We will explore what the Bible says about the subject.

Seventh, we will deal with love. Everything we have dealt with above can all be summed up in acts of love. We love the Lord and our fellow believers enough to want to serve them and see them treated well.

After we cover the above subjects, we will come back to our daily walk. We will see how all these thoughts bring about the complete work of Christ that brings about maturity and unity. There is a great deal of disunity because we do not want to work together to bring about the Kingdom of God on earth. We all want to go to Heaven, but we want to select who goes with us. In the last chapter, we will cover this.

SIMPLY NEW: WALK OF THE BELIEVER

CHAPTER SIX
BIBLE READING AND BIBLE STUDY

It is important to spend time in the Bible to properly grow and mature. It is necessary to find out what God has to say about different subjects that are important to our daily walk and growth.

We need to be careful not to take Scripture out of context lest we fall into error. We need to compare Scripture with Scripture so we can teach others the truth. Too often, we can fall into error by taking verses out of context as we build a doctrine on them.

SIMPLY NEW: WALK OF THE BELIEVER

Psalms 119:9-11: *Wherewithal shall a young man cleanse his way? by taking heed thereto according to thy word. With my whole heart have I sought thee: O let me not wander from thy commandments. Thy word have I hid in mine heart, that I might not sin against thee.*

Psalms 119:105: *Thy word is a lamp unto my feet, and a light unto my path.*

2 Timothy 2:14-16: *Of these things put them in rememberance, charging them before the Lord that they strive not about words to no profit, but to the subverting of the hearers. Study to shew thyself approved unto God, a workman that needeth not to be ashamed, rightly dividing the word of truth. But shun profane and vain babblings: for they will increase unto more ungodliness.*

    In these passages, we find out how important it is to get into the Bible and find out what it has to say. We are not to get into strife about the Bible—but rather study it to see what it has to say. We need to stay away from any wrong teaching that is simply babbling designed to confuse people. If we keep things in context and compare Scripture with Scripture, we will avoid many problems. As we study, we hide the Word in our hearts so we can avoid sin. This means we memorize the Word.

CHAPTER SIX: BIBLE READING AND BIBLE STUDY

Deuteronomy 17:18-20: *And it shall be, when he sitteth upon the throne of his kingdom, that he shall write him a copy of this law in a book out of that which is before the priests the Levites: And it shall be with him, and he shall read therein all the days of his life: that he may learn to fear the Lord his God, to keep all the words of this law and these statutes, to do them: That his heart be not lifted up above his brethren, and that he turn not aside from the commandment, to the right hand, or to the left: to the end that he may prolong his days in his kingdom, he, and his children, in the midst of Israel.*

Isaiah 34:16: *Seek ye out the book of the Lord and read: no one of these shall fail, none shall want her mate: for my mouth it hath commanded, and his spirit it hath gathered them.*

1 Timothy 4:12, 13: *Let no man despise thy youth; but be thou an example of the believers, in word, in conversation, in charity, in spirit, in faith, in purity. Till I come, give attendance to reading, to exhortation, to doctrine.*

We are not only to study on a daily basis, we are to read on a daily basis. Just as the King had to spend time in the Scripture, we are to do the same. Moses made it clear we are to spend time in the Word so we may grow in the Word and learn to fear (respect and reverence the Lord). This will keep us humble before the Lord.

Isaiah said we should seek out the Scripture and read it. In it we will find the commands of the Lord. The Spirit of God has spent time gathering the Word to help us to learn how to put Him first.

Paul told us not to worry about how young we are in the Lord. When we stay in the Word we can instruct others as we grow in the Faith. We grow in the things of the Lord to become pure and holy. Conversation here refers to lifestyle. Our lifestyle brings good results from knowing the Word.

2 Timothy 3:16, 17: *All scripture is given by inspiration of God, and is profitable for doctrine, for reproof, for correction, for instruction in righteousness that the man of God may be perfect, thoroughly furnished unto all good works.*

2 Peter 1:19-21: *We have also a more sure word of prophecy; whereunto ye do well that ye take heed, as unto a light that shineth in a dark place, until the day dawn, and the day star arise in your hearts: Knowing this first, that no prophecy of the scripture is of any private interpretation. For the prophecy came not in old time by the will of man: but holy men of God spake as they were moved by the*

CHAPTER SIX: BIBLE READING AND BIBLE STUDY

Holy Ghost.

As we see from these Scriptures, the Word of God is necessary for our lives. It is not to be privately interpreted, but checked with others who may know more than us. Scripture is important to us to help us understand how to grow and mature daily. We have nothing to be afraid of as we read and study the Word.

1 Corinthians 3:1, 2: *And I, brethren, could not speak unto you as unto spiritual, but as unto carnal, even as unto babes in Christ. I have fed you with milk, and not with meat: for hitherto ye were not able to bear it, neither yet now are ye able.*

Hebrews 5:11-14: *Of whom we have many things to say, and hard to be uttered, seeing ye are dull of hearing. For when for the time ye ought to be teachers, ye have need that one teach you again which be the first principles of the oracles of God; and are become such as have need of milk, and not of strong meat. For every one that useth milk is unskilful in the word of righteousness: for he is a babe. But strong meat belongeth to them that are of full age, even those who by reason of use have their senses exercised to discern both good and evil.*

SIMPLY NEW: WALK OF THE BELIEVER

1 Peter 2:1-3: *Wherefore laying aside all malice, and all guile, and hypocrisies, and envies, and all evil speakings, As newborn babes, desire the sincere milk of the word, that ye may grow thereby: If so be ye have tasted that the Lord is gracious.*

In these passages, we find out we are to desire the milk of the Word. Too often, though, mature or supposedly "mature believers" are still drinking the milk because they don't want to go on and really mature. They use the Word as a weapon to harm other believers and cause much damage. We need to stop that and really grow up so we can find out what is really in the Scripture.

Through all the verses shown in this chapter, we see the importance of spending time in the Word. There are many other verses and passages that tell us to get to know the Bible so we won't be led astray by false doctrine. We need to spend time reading the Bible daily.

I recommend a program that takes us through the Bible in a year. I believe it will give the reader a good grasp of what the Bible actually says and not what others may say. It must be consistent so the reader follows the pattern of the Scripture.

As we read the Bible, we need to understand and apply it. One good plan I

CHAPTER SIX: BIBLE READING AND BIBLE STUDY

have been introduced to is S.O.A.P. It helps us to examine chapters we read so we can apply it to our daily lives. What is S.O.A.P.? Let me explain it.

Scripture = Find a chapter in the Bible and read it in its entirety.

Observe = As you read, let the Holy Spirit guide you to a specific verse and observe what it says to you. Be careful not to take it out of context, but check the verses before and after it for a fuller understanding.

Apply = Once you observe it, apply it to your life.

Prayer = Pray over the verse and ask the Lord to help you apply it to your life.

Some other means of study are word studies, which is when the reader takes a word in the Scripture and run references to see how the word is used. A good concordance, either in the back of a Bible or a separate one, will give all the times the word is used. It helps to see how a word is used in light of the entire Bible. Chapter studies are often good in that the reader takes apart a chapter and sees how the writer is presenting the truth to them. Book studies help put everything in context. Breaking individual books down can cause the reader to understand the entire thought of the author of the book. There are other ways to study the Bible, but these are the primary ones that most people do.

Another thought: We can keep a journal of what we have read to see the progress we have made. This reveals how the Lord is speaking to us. Journals are good for writing down prayers and reading the Bible to see how the Lord wants to reveal Himself to us.

Remember, it is absolutely necessary to spend time in the Bible for us to truly grow. There are many false teachers out there who present half truths to convince the unwary to follow a specific teaching that leads to destruction. As we examine these teachings in light of the entire Bible, we find the errors. Study the Bible daily, no matter what.

CHAPTER SEVEN
PRAYER

As noted above, prayer is very simple. It is a two way communication between us and the Lord. While we need to talk, we also need to listen. We talk to the Lord like we talk to our best friend. We do not need to use "thees", "thous", or any part of the Elizabethan language. He understands the common language of people. We can ask questions, bring our concerns, and remind Him of His promises. The trick is, we have to be willing to listen so we can get answers. We may not like the answers we get, but we need to be open to what He has to say.

Sometimes the answer is yes. Sometimes the answer is no. Sometimes the answer is wait. It does not matter what the answer is, it is always for our ultimate good.

Jesus taught us a model prayer. We are going to break it down to learn how to pray. The disciples asked to be taught, so we can be taught. The prayer we are going to study may be familiar to us. Many churches use it as a "ritual prayer" that means nothing. The prayer is the Lord's Prayer. Let us look at it in its entirety before we break it down.

Matthew 6:9-13: _After this manner therefore pray ye: Our Father which art in heaven, Hallowed be thy name. Thy kingdom come. Thy will be done in earth, as it is in heaven. Give us this day our daily bread. And forgive us our debts, as we forgive our debtors. And lead us not into temptation, but deliver us from evil: For thine is the kingdom, and the power, and the glory, forever. Amen._

Luke 11:1-4: _And it came to pass, that, as he was praying in a certain place, when he ceased, one of his disciples said unto him, Lord, teach us to pray, as John also taught his disciples. And he said unto them, When ye pray, say, Our Father which art in heaven, Hallowed be thy name. Thy kingdom come. Thy will be done, as in heaven, so in earth. Give us day by day our daily bread. And_

CHAPTER SEVEN: PRAYER

forgive us our sins; for we also forgive every one that is indebted to us. And lead us not into temptation; but deliver us from evil.

Our Father which art in Heaven.

We need to acknowledge the Fathership of God. We must recognize He is our Father, not just some deity off in space that does not care for us. We know He lives in Heaven and we acknowledge He knows more than we could possibly ever know.

Isaiah 55:8-11: *For my thoughts are not your thoughts, neither are your ways my ways, saith the Lord. For as the heavens are higher than the earth, so are my ways higher than your ways, and my thoughts than your thoughts. For as the rain cometh down, and the snow from heaven, and returneth not thither, but watereth the earth, and maketh it bring forth and bud, that it may give seed to the sower, and bread to the eater: So shall my word be that goeth forth out of my mouth: it shall not return unto me void, but it shall accomplish that which I please, and it shall prosper in the thing whereto I sent it.*

The Lord's ways are much higher than ours. He knows the end from the beginning. He knows the outcome of our decisions before we do. Because of this, we can be assured He has our best interests at heart. When He tells us something, we can count on it because what He says will come to pass.

Hallowed be thy name.

We must acknowledge His holiness. He is a Holy God, and wants to lead us into holiness. During this portion, we acknowledge the great things He has done. We can speak of His creation, His power, His saving grace, and His teaching. We recognize that as He is holy, we are holy.

Leviticus 11:44: *For I am the Lord your God: ye shall therefore sanctify yourselves, and ye shall be holy; for I am holy: neither shall ye defile yourselves with any manner of creeping thing that creepeth upon the earth.*

We are to set ourselves apart to do what we need to do for the Lord. As we sanctify ourselves, we need to be holy because He is holy. We are not to defile ourselves with anything that would cause us to stumble or cause others to stumble.

CHAPTER SEVEN: PRAYER

Thy Kingdom come.

We want to see God's kingdom come down from Heaven and appear on earth. The Lord desires to show us what He wants on earth. The problem is, we often do not want to know what the plan is—we want to implement our own plans.

Psalms 22:27, 28: *All the ends of the world shall remember and turn unto the Lord: and all the kindreds of the nations shall worship before thee. the kingdom is the Lord's: and he is the governor among the nations.*

Psalms 103:19: *The Lord hath prepared his throne in the heavens; and his kingdom ruleth over all.*

Psalms 145:11-13: *They shall speak of the glory of thy kingdom, and talk of thy power; to make known to the sons of men his mighty acts, and the glorious majesty of his kingdom. Thy kingdom is an everlasting kingdom, and thy dominion endureth throughout all generations.*

It is important to acknowledge the Kingdom of God. He is in control of this world. We need to praise the Lord for His rulership. We need to pray the kingdom which is in Heaven down to this earth to take control from the enemy.

SIMPLY NEW: WALK OF THE BELIEVER

Thy will be done in earth as it is in heaven

We need to seek the Lord's will in our lives and in the lives of those around us. The Lord has a very specific will we can discover in the Bible for every circumstance. We need to realize the Lord has established His will in Heaven. He expects us to learn of it and bring it down to earth.

Daniel 4:34, 35: *And at the end of the days I Nebuchadnezzar lifted up mine eyes unto heaven, and mine understanding returned unto me, and I blessed the most High, and I praised and honoured him that liveth for ever, whose dominion is an everlasting dominion, and his kingdom is from generation to generation: And all the inhabitants of the earth are reputed as nothing: and he doeth according to his will in the army of heaven, and among the inhabitants of the earth: and none can stay his hand, or say unto him, What doest thou?*

Matthew 26:39-42: *And he went a little farther, and fell on his face, and prayed, saying, O my Father, if it be possible, let this cup pass from me: nevertheless not as I will, but as thou wilt. And he cometh unto the disciples, and findeth them asleep, and saith unto Peter, What, could ye not watch with me one hour? Watch and pray, that ye enter not*

CHAPTER SEVEN: PRAYER

into temptation: the spirit indeed is willing, but the flesh is weak. He went away again the second time, and prayed, saying, O my Father, if this cup may not pass away from me, except I drink it, thy will be done.

When we are not sure what the Father wants, we need to seek Him and ask. The Scripture gives some very specific things that are His will. When Jesus prayed in the garden, He sought the will of the Father in the taking of the cup. He knew He had to die, but His flesh rebelled. We often know what the Father wants, but we don't want to face it. We need to seek the will of the Father in our daily lives, no matter how painful it may be. The Lord knows the final outcome in every situation.

Give us this day our daily bread.

We are told here we can bring our petitions and desires. We need to realize it is not just physical needs. It is also emotional, mental, and spiritual needs. We need to understand the Father gives us what we need for the current day, not for a long period of time.

Exodus 16:4, 5: *Then said the Lord unto Moses, Behold, I will rain bread from heaven for you; and the people shall go out and* gather a certain rate every day, that I may prove them, whether they will walk in my law or no. And it shall come to pass, that on the sixth day they shall prepare that which they bring in; and it shall be twice as much as they gather daily.

Proverbs 30:7-9: *Two things have I required of thee: deny me them not before I die: remove far from me vanity and lies: give me neither poverty nor riches; feed me with food convenient for me: lest I be full, and deny thee, and say, Who is the Lord? Or lest I be poor and steal, and take the name of my God in vain.*

Isaiah 33:15, 16: *He that walketh righteously, and speaketh uprightly; he that despiseth the gain of oppressions that shaketh his hands from holding of bribes, that stoppeth his ears from hearing of blood, and shutteth his eyes from seeing evil; he shall dwell on high: his place of defense shall be the munitions of rocks: bread shall be given him; his waters shall be sure.*

      The Lord gave manna to the children of Israel on a daily basis. He wanted to prove them to see if they would obey Him. We know from reading further, they disobeyed and learned the hard way to obey the Lord. We need to seek to be satisfied with what the Lord gives us on a daily basis. We must not complain about what we receive. We should be grateful for what we have. We are assured we will receive what we need as we serve the Lord and refuse to participate in things that are wrong.

Forgive us our debts as we forgive our debtors.

If we want forgiveness, we must extend it. Forgiveness is a commandment, not a request. When we refuse to forgive, we set ourselves up for failure and disappointment. We choose to walk in bitterness, holding grudges. When we do, we wonder why we can't find the forgiveness we so desperately want. The prayer is very specific. If you don't forgive, you will not be forgiven.

And lead us not into temptation, but deliver us from evil.

While it is true God does not tempt us, we need to recognize the enemy tempts us with evil. We seek help from the Lord to avoid evil or be set free from evil. We are tempted to do things that displease the Lord, but we need to remember two things. (1) We will never be tempted above what we can handle. (2) We are provided a way of escape.

James 1:13-15: Let no man say when he is tempted, I am tempted of God: for God cannot be tempted with evil, neither tempteth he any man: But every man is tempted, when he is drawn away of his own lust, and enticed. Then when lust hath conceived, it bringeth forth sin: and sin, when it is finished, bringeth forth death.

1 Corinthians 10:13: There hath no temptation taken you but such as is common to man: but God is faithful, who will not suffer you to be tempted above that ye are able; but will with the temptation also make a way to escape, that ye may be able to bear it.

2 Corinthians 12:7-9: And lest I should be exalted above measure through the abundance of the revelations, there was given to me a thorn in the flesh, the messenger of Satan to buffet me, lest I should be exalted above measure. For this thing I besought the Lord thrice, that it might depart from me. And he said unto me, My grace is sufficient for thee: for my strength is made perfect in weakness. Most gladly therefore will I rather glory in my infirmities, that the power of Christ may rest upon me.

2 Peter 2:9: The Lord knoweth how to deliver the godly out of temptations, and to reserve the unjust unto the day of judgment to be punished:

CHAPTER SEVEN: PRAYER

These passages tell us where temptation comes from and how to handle it. Temptation comes from an evil desire that keeps us from serving the Lord. This temptation (if acted upon) leads to sin which leads to death. We know they will come, but we can resist and escape them if we choose to obey the Lord. Understand, when we are tempted, we are not tempted above what the Lord believes we are capable of. He also provides a way to escape so we do not fall for it. Many times, we are given knowledge of how to walk the walk in a deeper way. We are placed in a difficult place—knowing we can rejoice because His grace is sufficient for us. The Lord knows how to deliver us because we are godly, but we must be willing to be delivered.

The Lord knows how to deliver us because we are godly, but we must be willing to be delivered.

For Thine is the Kingdom, and the Power, and the Glory forever, amen.

Once we have dealt with all the issues, we rejoice that we are heard. We acknowledge the fact that the Lord is in charge, full of power and full of glory. We must remember, we need to acknowledge the power of the Lord to do what we have asked.

When we pray, ask all in the name

of Jesus. He has given us His name to approach the Father. No matter what we ask in His name. He promised to answer our requests!

John 14:13, 14: *And whatsoever ye shall ask in my name, that will I do, that the Father may be glorified in the Son. If ye shall ask any thing in my name, I will do it.*

John 15:16: *Ye have not chosen me, but I have chosen you, and ordained you, that ye should go and bring forth fruit, and that your fruit should remain: that whatsoever ye shall ask of the Father in my name, he may give it you.*

John 16:23, 24: *And in that day ye shall ask me nothing. Verily, verily, I say unto you, Whatsoever ye shall ask the Father in my name, he will give it you. Hitherto have ye asked nothing in my name: ask and ye shall receive, that your joy may be full.*

Jesus made it abundantly clear, we are to ask in His name. We speak to the Father in His name and we can expect an answer. He has chosen us and set us apart to go out and bring in fruit. This fruit are the souls we bring into the Kingdom. We can ask the Father for souls to be brought in and expect Him to answer. This brings us great joy knowing our

CHAPTER SEVEN: PRAYER

needs are met and we are doing the will of the Father.

As mentioned in chapter six, we should keep a journal of prayer requests and answers. When we do this, we can have a visual means of seeing how God answers prayer. A daily record helps us stay on track. Part of journaling is recording anything the Lord says to us specifically about different issues. When we read these comments, we are encouraged to keep on going, as we grow and mature.

SIMPLY NEW: WALK OF THE BELIEVER

CHAPTER EIGHT
CHURCH ATTENDANCE

We are called to be a body of believers—not lone rangers. When we refuse to fellowship with other believers, we are saying, "God made a mistake" when He brought others to Himself. It almost puts us above the Lord in how we deal with them. We may have been hurt and suffered at the hands of fellow believers, but we need to keep going. If we ask, the Lord will lead us to the right fellowship that will minister to us and help heal us from past hurts.

Psalms 122:1: _I was glad when they said unto me, Let us go into the house of the Lord_

Hebrews 10:23-25: _Let us hold fast the profession of our faith without wavering; (for he is faithful that promised,) and let us consider one another to provoke unto love and to good works: not forsaking the assembling of ourselves together, as the manner of some is, but exhorting one another: and so much the more, as ye see the day approaching._

David said he was glad when he went to the house of God. He knew where his help was. We can rejoice when we attend church because we recognize that's where our help is. We are exhorted to attend church so we might encourage and exhort one another.

Someone may argue that it does not matter where we fellowship. I say it does matter. We must fellowship where the Lord wants us to fellowship.

Matthew 18:19, 20: _Again I say unto you, That if two of you shall agree on earth as touching anything that they shall ask, it shall_

CHAPTER EIGHT: CHURCH ATTENDANCE

be done for them of my Father which is in heaven. For where two or three are gathered together in my name, there am I in the midst of them

We are told to be in agreement with one another so the Father will answer us. When we gather in the name of Jesus, He is in the midst of us. The church we attend must be one where there is agreement and unity. It must put Jesus first and foremost. We must be sure the teaching is the full Gospel—that it puts emphasis on the Word of God.

<u>1 Corinthians 3:6-9:</u> *I have planted, Apollos watered; but God gave the increase. So then neither is he that planteth any thing, neither he that watereth; but God that giveth the increase. Now he that planteth and he that watereth are one: and every man shall receive his own reward according to his own labour. For we are labourers together with God: ye are God's husbandry, ye are God's building.*

When we spend time in the church God placed us, we can grow. We are planted so we may be watered. While this is referring to witnessing, it can also apply to attending church. The minister we are under keeps helping us grow and mature. We should never be afraid to go to the leader for help when we are in trouble or do not understand things in the Word.

What can we expect when we attend church? We can expect a time of worship, a time of prayer, a time of communion, a time to receive offerings, a time of message, and a time of an altar call. These elements are necessary to bring us into the presence of the Lord to hear what He has to say. Let's explore these areas.

Worship

After opening prayer, it is important to come into the presence of God in praise and worship. This is usually a time of corporate singing. We have to be open to the Holy Spirit to do what He wants.

Ephesians 5:19-21: *Speaking to yourselves in psalms and hymns and spiritual songs, singing and making melody in your heart to the Lord; Giving thanks always for all things unto God and the Father in the name of our Lord Jesus Christ; Submitting yourselves one to another in the fear of God.*

Colossians 3:16: *Let the word of Christ dwell in you richly in all wisdom; teaching and admonishing one another in psalms and hymns and spiritual songs, singing with grace*

CHAPTER EIGHT: CHURCH ATTENDANCE

in your hearts to the Lord.

It is important to spend time in worship. We encourage one another with the music we offer to the Lord. It does not matter what type of music we offer as long as it glorifies the Lord and edifies the body.

<u>Psalms 33:3:</u> *Sing unto him a new song; play skillfully with a loud noise.*

<u>Psalms 96:1:</u> *O sing unto the Lord a new song: sing unto the Lord, all the earth.*

<u>Psalms 149:1:</u> *Praise ye the Lord. Sing unto the Lord a new song, and his praise in the congregation of saints*

Over and over David, (the Psalmist) tells us to sing and praise the Lord. All the way through the psalms we read of encouragement to praise the Lord as we remember His mighty works. It is important to spend time in praise and worship.

Prayer

After we spend time in worship, we need to spend time in prayer. This is a time of approaching the Lord to present the needs and wants of the body. We must honor the Lord no matter what.

Philippians 4:6: *Be careful for nothing; but in everything by prayer and supplication with thanksgiving let your requests be made known unto God.*

Paul instructs us how to pray for one another. We are to make requests but also spend time in thanksgiving to the Lord. The implication is: We can bring everything to God and expect an answer.

Communion

Communion is also known as the Lord's Supper. The Scripture says we need to do this often. Some churches do it once a week. Some do it once a month. Some do it when they think about it. Some don't do it at all or seem not to do it at all. These last ones violate the Scripture. It does not matter when we take communion; it matters that we do.

1 Corinthians 11:23-26: *For I have received of the Lord that which also I delivered unto you, that the Lord Jesus the same night in which he was betrayed took bread: And when*

CHAPTER EIGHT: CHURCH ATTENDANCE

he had given thanks, he brake it, and said, Take, eat: this is my body, which is broken for you: this do in remembrance of me. After the same manner also he took the cup, when he had supped, saying, this cup is the new testament in my blood: this do ye, as oft as ye drink it, in remembrance of me. For as often as ye eat this bread, and drink this cup, ye do shew the Lord's death till he come.

    This familiar passage tells us how to proceed with the communion. Each of the Gospels tells us how the Lord Jesus implemented the supper. Paul simply summarized what was said in the Gospel. He spends time in 1 Corinthians 11, telling us we are to examine ourselves to make sure we are taking communion worthily. Often there is a speaker who helps us to examine ourselves with brief thoughts on taking communion. Even if there is not, we need to pray and make sure we are in line with the Word of God —that there is no overt sin in us before we partake. We need to make sure it is not just a ritual that we have to go through to please the Lord.

Giving

    While we have an entire chapter on giving, it is important to give to the work of the ministry. We may start small, but we need to be sure we move up to full tithes and offerings. We need to understand churches need the money to take care of expenses. We are not just giving to the church; we are giving to the Lord.

Sermon

After we have ministered to the Lord in the various elements of the service, He wants to minister back to us. He uses the minister to give us thoughts to live by. The pastor or minister spends time in the Word to bring us what the Lord wants us to know.

Colossians 1:25-29: *Whereof I am made a minister, according to the dispensation of God which is given to me for you, to fulfil the word of God; Even the mystery which hath been hid from ages and from generations, but now is made manifest to his saints: To whom God would make known what is the riches of the glory of this mystery among the Gentiles; which is Christ in you, the hope of glory: Whom we preach, warning every man, and teaching every man in all wisdom; that we may present every man perfect in Christ Jesus: Whereunto I also labour, striving according to his working, which worketh in me mightily.*

CHAPTER EIGHT: CHURCH ATTENDANCE

Paul makes it clear how we are to preach and communicate what the Lord wants to say. All sermons need to follow the Scripture and not take anything out of context. They are designed to exhort and encourage the believer.

We, who listen to the messages, need to examine our Bibles to see if the minister is speaking the Word accurately. It would be a good idea to take notes during the sermon to review later. If we just take down the verses, we can examine them later to see how the verses compare to what else the Bible says.

Altar call

Once we listen to the message, we need to respond to it. We need to take the opportunity to go to the altar before the Lord to repent or rejoice in the things He has shown us. The minister calls for a response. Some come to accept the Lord. Some come to receive healing. Others come out of conviction. The point is they come.

James 5:13-16: *Is any among you afflicted? Let him pray. Is any merry? Let him sing psalms. Is any sick among you? Let him call for the elders of the church; and let them pray over him, anointing him with oil in the name of the Lord: and the prayer of faith shall save the* *sick, and the Lord shall raise him up; and if he have committed sins, they shall be forgiven him. Confess your faults one to another, and pray for one another, that ye may be healed. The effectual fervent prayer of a righteous man availeth much.*

James gives a perfect outline of an altar call. He covers the elements necessary to minister to the body. We need to realize the minister can't do it all alone; he needs elders to help him pray. The minister needs altar workers to guide people to the leaders so they can be ministered to. As we do this, we will find many people will be ministered to.

As we can see, we need to have decency and order in the service. This plan gives that order. Now we must be open to the Holy Spirit to change the order as necessary to reach someone, but in general, it is helpful for us to know what to expect.

1 Corinthians 14:26, 40: How is it then, brethren? When ye come together, everyone of you hath a psalm, hath a doctrine, hath a tongue, hath a revelation, hath an interpretation. Let all things be done unto edifying…Let all things be done decently and in order.

CHAPTER EIGHT: CHURCH ATTENDANCE

Everyone has something to share to edify the body. When the Spirit moves, He helps us to learn from one another. He does not do things in such a way as to cause confusion. He expects us to keep order. This encourages us to minister to one another. As we do this, we grow and mature in the Lord. Let us not forsake the attendance of the local body of believers in church.

SIMPLY NEW: WALK OF THE BELIEVER

CHAPTER NINE
GIVING

We need to give to the Lord. We give tithes and offerings to Him. It is a command of the Lord. We generally give to the church where we attend so we can support the ministry. Many try to say we don't have to do that, the church should not ask for money. The problem is, it takes money to run any ministry. Businesses or utilities companies are not going to give free services to the church. To assume so, makes the person who says that a fool.

Genesis 14:18-20: And Melchizedek king of Salem brought forth bread and wine: and he was the priest of the most high God. And he blessed him, and said Blessed be Abram of the most high God, possessor of heaven and earth: And blessed be the most high God, which hath delivered thine enemies into thy hand. And he gave him tithes of all.

Deuteronomy 12:5-7: But unto the place which the Lord your God shall choose out of all your tribes to put his name there, even unto his habitation shall ye seek, and thither thou shalt come: And thither ye shall bring your burnt offerings, and your sacrifices, and your tithes, and heave offerings of your hand, and your vows, and your freewill offerings, and the firstlings of your herds and of your flocks: And there ye shall eat before the Lord your God, and ye shall rejoice in all that ye put your hand unto, ye and your households, wherein the Lord thy God hath blessed thee.

Deuteronomy 12: 10-12: But when ye go over Jordan, and dwell in the land which the Lord your God giveth you to inherit, and when he giveth you rest from all your enemies round about, so that ye dwell in safety; Then there shall be a place which the Lord your God shall choose to cause his name to dwell there; thither shall ye bring all that I command you; your burnt offerings, and your sacrifices, your tithes, and the heave offering of your hand, and all your choice vows which ye vow

CHAPTER NINE: GIVING

unto the Lord: And ye shall rejoice before the Lord your God, ye, and your sons, and your daughters, and your menservants, and your maidservants, and the Levite that is within your gates; forasmuch as he hath no part nor inheritance with you.

Tithes are very important to God. He designated where He wants His tithes and offerings to be given. In the Old Testament, it was the tabernacle and the temple. Today, it is the local church. He did it to support the ministry He designated.

Now we will deal with offerings. These are moneys and items given above the tithes. They are freewill offerings, meaning they are not ordered by the Lord but given from the heart. It is important to remember to give as the Lord blesses us.

Exodus 36:2-6: *And Moses called Bezaleel and Aholiab, and every wise hearted man, in whose heart the Lord had put wisdom, even every one whose heart stirred him up to come unto the work to do it: And they received of Moses all the offering, which the children of Israel had brought for the work of the service of the sanctuary, to make it withal. And they brought yet unto him free offerings every morning. And all the wise men, that wrought all the work of the sanctuary, came every man* *from his work which they made; and they spake unto Moses, saying, The people bring much more than enough for the service of the work, which the Lord commanded to make. And Moses gave commandment, and they caused it to be proclaimed throughout the camp, saying, Let neither man nor woman make any more work for the offering of the sanctuary. So the people were restrained from bringing.*

2 Corinthians 9:6, 7: *But this I say, He which soweth sparingly shall reap also sparingly; and he which soweth bountifully shall reap also bountifully. Every man according as he purposeth in his heart, so let him give; not grudgingly, or of necessity: for God loveth a cheerful giver.*

It is clear, the Lord desires our offerings. We need to give as the Lord gives to us. We are to be cheerful givers. In Exodus, the people gave so much they had to be restrained from giving to build the tabernacle. Somewhere in the Old Testament there is another story where the people had to be restrained because they gave too much. That's a good problem to have. In the meantime, we need to give offerings on a regular basis. We see from Scripture, if we give, we will receive back what we have given. We find there is a curse from not giving to the Lord. The children of Israel gave the

CHAPTER NINE: GIVING

worst of their goods to the Lord or they simply didn't give. If we want the blessings of God, we need to give.

Malachi 1:6-8: *A son honoureth his father, and a servant his master: if then I be a father, where is mine honour? and if I be a master, where is my fear? saith the Lord of hosts unto you, O priests, that despise my name. And ye say, Wherein have we despised thy name? Ye offer polluted bread upon mine altar; and ye say, Wherein have we polluted thee? In that ye say, The table of the Lord is contemptible. And if ye offer the blind for sacrifice, is it not evil? and if ye offer the lame and sick, is it not evil? offer it now unto thy governor; will he be pleased with thee, or accept thy person? saith the Lord of hosts.*

Malachi 3:8-11: *Will a man rob God? Yet ye have robbed me. But ye say, Wherein have we robbed thee? In tithes and offerings. Ye are cursed with a curse: for ye have robbed me, even this whole nation. Bring ye all the tithes into the storehouse, that there may be meat in mine house, and prove me now herewith, saith the Lord of hosts, if I will not open you the windows of heaven, and pour you out a blessing, that there shall not be room enough to receive it. And I will rebuke the devourer for your sakes, and he shall not destroy the fruits of your ground; neither shall your vine cast her fruit before the time in the field, saith the Lord* *of hosts.*

As we can see from these passages, it is important to give our best to the Lord. We are not to make excuses or justify why we don't. If we want to see the blessing of the Lord, we will give our best in all we receive. The storehouse mentioned here is the local church. The Lord wants His ministers taken care of.

Not only are we to give to the local church, but we are to help the less fortunate. Jesus called these offerings, "alms." We need to obey the Lord in helping others. Many don't need a hand out, they need a hand up. Those who seek a hand out are not really trying to get out of the mess they are in. We are to help those locally as well as overseas.

Matthew 6:1-4: *Take heed that ye do not your alms before men, to be seen of them: otherwise ye have no reward of your Father which is in heaven. Therefore when thou doest thine alms, do not sound a trumpet before thee, as the hypocrites do in the synagogues and in the streets, that they may have glory of men. Verily I say unto you, They have their reward. But when thou doest alms, let not thy left hand know what thy right hand doeth: That thine alms may be in secret: and thy Father which seeth in secret himself shall*

CHAPTER NINE: GIVING

reward thee openly.

     We are warned to not make a public spectacle in our giving. We need to be quiet and operate in secret. The religious leaders and people often make it a point to tell everyone what they did. We see it today. Many televangelists spend much time telling the world what they are doing. Some may do it with pureness of heart, others are blowing a trumpet. We need to be careful and seek the Lord as to what we are to do.

     Let us give unto the Lord in a way that blesses Him. We need to be sure we do what the Lord wants in our daily lives.

SIMPLY NEW: WALK OF THE BELIEVER

CHAPTER TEN
HEALING

The Bible teaches healing of the body, mind, emotions, and spirit. Jesus healed all who came to Him. The disciples healed as well. Healing is not just for the past, it is for the present. Many people are being healed today. Faith is an element of healing. It is one of the signs that follow believers.

<u>Matthew 10:7, 8:</u> *And as you go, preach, saying, The kingdom of heaven is at hand. Heal the sick, cleanse the lepers, raise the dead,* cast out devils: freely ye have received, freely give.*

Mark 16:17, 18: *And these signs shall follow them that believe; In my name shall they cast out devils; they shall speak with new tongues; They shall take up serpents; and if they drink any deadly thing, it shall not hurt them; they shall lay hands on the sick, and they shall recover.*

Luke 10:8, 9: *And into whatsoever city ye enter, and they receive you, eat such things as are set before you: And heal the sick that are therein, and say unto them, The kingdom of God is come nigh unto you.*

In these passages, we see Jesus' command to heal the sick. We are to obey the Lord in this. It is a part of declaring the Kingdom of God is at hand. Part of healing involves the casting out of demons. We have freely received the blessing of the Lord so we are to give it out. Any believer can do this, it is not reserved to just a select few.

In Mark 16, when it talks about serpents and drinking any deadly thing, it does not mean deliberately doing the thing. It is talking about the accidental doing of the thing. To do it deliberately is to put God to a foolish test. There is no guarantee He will heal us when we do this thing.

CHAPTER TEN: HEALING

Let us look at some examples of healing. The Gospels are full of stories of healing. We are going to look at the woman healed of the issue of blood, healing of the centurion's servant, and the healing of the Syrophoenician's daughter. It makes the point that faith is required for healing.

<u>Mark 5:25-34:</u> *And a certain woman, which had an issue of blood twelve years, And had suffered many things of many physicians, and had spent all that she had, and was nothing bettered, but rather grew worse, When she had heard of Jesus, came in the press behind, and touched his garment. For she said, If I may touch but his clothes, I shall be whole. And straightway the fountain of her blood was dried up; and she felt in her body that she was healed of that plague. Jesus, immediately knowing in himself that virtue had gone out of him, turned him about in the press, and said, Who touched my clothes? And his disciples said unto him, Thou seest the multitude thronging thee, and sayest thou, Who touched me? And he looked round about to see her that had done this thing. But the woman fearing and trembling, knowing what was done in her, came and fell down before him, and told him all the truth. And he said unto her, Daughter, thy faith hath made thee whole; go in peace, and be whole of thy plague.*

SIMPLY NEW: WALK OF THE BELIEVER

Luke 7:2-10: *And a certain centurion's servant, who was dear unto him, was sick, and ready to die. And when he heard of Jesus, he sent unto him the elders of the Jews, beseeching him that he would come and heal his servant. And when they came to Jesus, they besought him instantly, saying, That he was worthy for whom he should do this: For he loveth our nation, and he hath built us a synagogue. Then Jesus went with them. And when he was now not far from the house, the centurion sent friends to him, saying unto him, Lord, trouble not thyself: for I am not worthy that thou shouldest enter under my roof: Wherefore neither thought I myself worthy to come unto thee: but say in a word, and my servant shall be healed. For I also am a man set under authority, having under me soldiers, and I say unto one, Go, and he goeth; and to another, Come, and he cometh; and to my servant, Do this, and he doeth it. When Jesus heard these things, he marvelled at him, and turned him about, and said unto the people that followed him, I say unto you, I have not found so great faith, no, not in Israel. And they that were sent, returning to the house, found the servant whole that had been sick.*

Matthew 15:22-28: *And, behold, a woman of Canaan came out of the same coasts, and cried unto him, saying, Have mercy on me, O Lord, thou son of David; my daughter is grievously vexed with a devil. But he answered her not a word. And his disciples came and*

CHAPTER TEN: HEALING

besought him, saying, Send her away; for she crieth after us. But he answered and said, I am not sent but unto the lost sheep of the house of Israel. Then came she and worshipped him, saying, Lord, help me. But he answered and said, It is not meet to take the children's bread, and to cast it to dogs. And she said, Truth, Lord: yet the dogs eat of the crumbs which fall from their masters' table. Then Jesus answered and said unto her, O woman, great is thy faith: be it unto thee even as thou wilt. And her daughter was made whole from that very hour.

Mark 7:25-30: *For a certain woman, whose young daughter had an unclean spirit, heard of him, and came and fell at his feet: the woman was a Greek, a Syrophenician by nation; and she besought him that he would cast forth the devil out of her daughter: But Jesus said unto her, Let the children first be filled; for it is not meet to take the children's bread, and to cast it to the dogs. And she answered and said unto him, Yes Lord, yet the dogs under the table eat the children's crumbs. And he said unto her, for this saying: go thy way, the devil is gone out of thy daughter. And when she was come to her house, she found the devil gone out and her daughter laid upon the bed.*

In each of these passages, we find a serious problem. The person or someone close to the person, has a serious illness. He or she goes to Jesus for help. The need is met. Faith is exercised which leads to healing and deliverance. It is obvious faith is necessary for healing. In every case listed in the Gospels, faith was exercised by the person coming to Jesus.

Matthew 13:54-58: *And when he was come into his own country, he taught them in their synagogue, insomuch that they were astonished, and said, Whence hath this man this wisdom, and these mighty works? Is not this the carpenter's son? is not his mother called Mary? and his brethren, James, and Joses, and Simon, and Judas? And his sisters, are they not all with us? Whence then hath this man all these things? And they were offended in him. But Jesus said unto them, A prophet is not without honour, save in his own country, and in his own house. And he did not many mighty works there because of their unbelief.*

    We see in this passage, Jesus went to His own country to minister to them. The people refused to listen, and became offended. Because of this, Jesus could not do anything for them. Mark in telling the same story. He mentions, "Jesus did no mighty works save He laid His hands on a few sick folks and healed them." It was lack of

CHAPTER TEN: HEALING

faith that caused the people to fail to receive what Jesus had for them.

Today, many come to Jesus for healing, but are not healed. There are no real answers as to why. Some may say it was a lack of faith. I venture the opinion it may be that the Lord knows if they were healed they would return to their sin. Some die in their illness. They receive the ultimate healing.

Some are not healed because they are taught healing has passed away. This is a form of unbelief. Healing has not passed away—it is available for those who desire it, if the Lord allows it. We need to be careful to not condemn those who are not healed when they ask for it. We need to have compassion for them, pray for them, and stand by them.

One thing we can do is find Scriptures that apply to our situation and quote them. We need to do this by faith. Be careful to not make it a ritual. Another thing to do is seek the Lord for His ultimate will in our lives for the situation we are facing. Sometimes, it is a good idea to simply relax and allow the Lord to do what He wants.

SIMPLY NEW: WALK OF THE BELIEVER

HE TOUCHED ME

Shackled by a heavy burden

'Neath a load of guilt and shame

Then the hand of Jesus touched me

And now i am no longer the same

He touched, oh, he touched me

And oh the joy that floods my soul!

Something happened, and now i know

He touched me, and made me whole

Since I've met this blessed savior

Since he's cleansed and made me whole

I'll never cease to praise him

I'll shout it while eternity rolls

Oh! he touched me! Oh! he touched me!

He touched me! And Oh the joy that floods my soul!

Something happened, and now i know

He touched me, and made me whole

CHAPTER ELEVEN
FORGIVENESS

The Bible is very clear. We must forgive others regardless of what has been done to us. Jesus died on the cross as an innocent man.

Luke 23:34: *Then said Jesus, Father, forgive them; for they know not what they do. And they parted his raiment, and cast lots.*

As we can see from this verse, Jesus forgave His tormentors. He was arrested, beaten, whipped, forced to carry His own cross, and nailed to it. He was and is our sacrificial Lamb. The religious leaders saw Him as a threat because He was king over them. Pilate and Rome wanted peace any way they could get it. They conspired together to destroy the obvious threat to what they wanted in life.

 I do not believe anyone has ever suffered to the depth and extent Jesus suffered. We all have suffered hurt, rejection, and betrayal. We have become damaged by life. I am not saying we have not suffered, but not to the extent to what Jesus went through when He suffered from our sins.

 Just as Jesus forgave those who abused, misused, and killed Him, so we must forgive those who have done the same things to us. Forgiveness is not an option based on how we feel about the person or situation. It is a command we must obey if we wish to grow in our maturity.

 What does forgiveness mean? According to Vine's Dictionary, forgiveness means to send forth; send away; to remit; debts, these being completely canceled sins. It signifies remission of the punishment due to sinful conduct. The deliverance of the sinner from the penalty imposed. It involves the complete removal of the cause of offenses. In other words, it is the total removal of offenses and sins from our hearts. It is letting

CHAPTER ELEVEN: FORGIVENESS

go of offense, no matter what the cause.

Forgiveness does not benefit the person who offended us. It benefits us. I heard someone say, "Unforgiveness is like drinking poison and expecting the offender to die." (It is you that will die, not the offender.) We need to extend forgiveness regardless of whom it is.

I can hear protests being made. If we don't punish the offender, he will get off scot-free. Actually, when we forgive, we turn them over to the Lord for Him to deal with them. Besides, it is not our place to worry about that. In reality, the offender is not overly concerned, let alone cares. Often the offender is not even aware of the offense. All we have to do is be obedient and let the Lord handle the offender.

In the following pages is a word study I did on forgiveness. I hope this study will help you understand forgiveness.

National Sin.

Exodus 32:31-33: *And Moses returned unto the Lord, and said, Oh, this people have sinned a great sin, and have made them gods of gold. Yet now, if thou wilt forgive their sin--; and if not, blot me, I pray thee, out of thy book which thou hast written. And the Lord said unto Moses, Whosoever hath sinned* *against me, him will I blot out of my book.*

Moses interceded for the sin of the people. He asked God to forgive the people's sin. He went on to say if God would not, he wanted his name blotted out of God's book. We need to realize as we intercede for others, we can claim the same promise.

1 Kings 8:30-40: *And hearken thou to the supplication of thy servant, and of thy people Israel, when they shall pray toward this place: and hear thou in heaven thy dwelling place: and when thou hearest, forgive. If any man trespass against his neighbour, and an oath be laid upon him to cause him to swear, and the oath come before thine altar in this house: Then hear thou in heaven, and do, and judge thy servants, condemning the wicked, to bring his way upon his head; and justifying the righteous, to give him according to his righteousness. When thy people Israel be smitten down before the enemy, because they have sinned against thee, and shall turn again to thee, and confess thy name, and pray, and make supplication unto thee in this house: Then hear thou in heaven, and forgive the sin of thy people Israel, and bring them again unto the land which thou gavest unto their fathers. When heaven is shut up, and there is no rain, because they have sinned*

CHAPTER ELEVEN: FORGIVENESS

against thee; if they pray toward this place, and confess thy name, and turn from their sin, when thou afflictest them: Then hear thou in heaven, and forgive the sin of thy servants, and of thy people Israel, that thou teach them the good way wherein they should walk, and give rain upon thy land, which thou hast given to thy people for an inheritance. If there be in the land famine, if there be pestilence, blasting, mildew, locust, or if there be caterpiller; if their enemy besiege them in the land of their cities; whatsoever plague, whatsoever sickness there be; What prayer and supplication soever be made by any man, or by all thy people Israel, which shall know every man the plague of his own heart, and spread forth his hands toward this house: Then hear thou in heaven thy dwelling place, and forgive, and do, and give to every man according to his ways, whose heart thou knowest; (for thou, even thou only, knowest the hearts of all the children of men;) That they may fear thee all the days that they live in the land which thou gavest unto our fathers.

Solomon prayed for the people of Israel at the dedication of the temple. He asked the Lord to forgive the people's sin. He mentioned specific conditions that would arise because of the sin. He asked if the people repented and asked for mercy, would God forgive the people? We know God heard and responded by saying He would.

No matter what happens, we need to repent and seek forgiveness. As we do we will be delivered.

2 Chronicles 7:14: *If my people, which are called by my name, shall humble themselves, and pray, and seek my face, and turn from their wicked ways; then will I hear from heaven, and will forgive their sin, and will heal their land.*

    God responded to Solomon's prayer. He told him if the people would repent from sin and seek Him with all their hearts, God would hear and forgive them. We need to turn to God in our sin and distress. We will be forgiven and healed. The problem is we don't and suffer for it. We need to come to a place of repentance daily.

    In these three Scriptures listed above, the Lord is dealing with national sin. God is calling one person or a group of people to intercede for the nation. The person responsible to intercede is the leader of the nation. He must be humble enough to admit the sin and to petition God. If the leader refuses, the Lord will call people to pray for the leader and the country.

CHAPTER ELEVEN: FORGIVENESS

Personal Sin.

Exodus 34:6, 7: *And the Lord passed by before him, and proclaimed, The Lord, The Lord God, merciful and gracious, longsuffering, and abundant in goodness and truth, Keeping mercy for thousands, forgiving iniquity and transgression and sin, and that will by no means clear the guilty; visiting the iniquity of the fathers upon the children, and upon the children's children, unto the third and to the fourth generation.*

God wants to have mercy on all who seek Him. He extends forgiveness, and shows His love to all who come to Him. Yet, if people don't they won't be forgiven — but will allow that sin to fall upon future generations. The decision is up to each individual. Too often, though, people don't believe it. They go on sinning. They go on to see problems they can't explain in their families. They need to repent and get their lives right thus short-circuiting the curse.

Psalms 32:1: *Blessed is he whose transgression is forgiven, whose sin is covered.*

We are blessed or happy when we are forgiven of our transgressions.

Transgressions are the act of passing over or beyond any law or rule of moral duty, the violation of a law or known principle of rectitude or breach of command. In other words, when we break the law, we are disobeying the Lord. We need to repent and seek God. As we admit we broke the law we are forgiven and set free from bondage.

Psalms 86:5: *For thou, Lord, art good, and ready to forgive; and plenteous in mercy unto all them that call upon thee*

David says the Lord desires to forgive and is merciful to those who seek Him. We need to seek the Lord daily in times of trouble. As we confess our sins, the Lord is quick to forgive us. He shows mercy to us because He loves us.

Psalms 103:2-5: *Bless the Lord, O my soul, and forget not all his benefits: Who forgiveth all thine iniquities; who healeth all thy diseases; Who redeemeth thy life from destruction; who crowneth thee with lovingkindness and tender mercies; Who satisfieth thy mouth with good things; so that thy youth is renewed like the eagle's.*

CHAPTER ELEVEN: FORGIVENESS

We need to remember the benefits of the Lord. We are to command ourselves to be happy. The reason we can be is that He forgives our iniquities and heals our diseases. Iniquity is injustice; unrighteousness; want of rectitude in principle; a particular deviation of rectitude; a sin in crime; wickedness; any act of injustice; original want of holiness or depravity. He forgives all of our behavior and changes us as necessary.

We are dealing with personal sin. It is impossible to realize we are forgiven for all the wrong we have done. We can count on the Lord to forgive us if we confess our sin. The problem is we often don't want to because we don't want to admit our sin. We need to stop making excuses so we can be forgiven.

Forgiving One Another.

Matthew 6:12, 14, 15: *And forgive us our debts, as we forgive our debtors. For if ye forgive men their trespasses, your heavenly Father will also forgive you: But if ye forgive not men their trespasses, neither will your Father forgive your trespasses.*

We are commanded to forgive one another if we want to be forgiven. In the Lord's Prayer it is a request. Later Jesus told us the consequences of refusing to forgive. If we don't want forgiveness we hold on to bitterness and unforgiveness. If that is how we want to live, we will be miserable. Instead, we need to forgive.

Matthew 9:2-7: *And, behold, they brought to him a man sick of the palsy, lying on a bed: and Jesus seeing their faith said unto the sick of the palsy; Son, be of good cheer; thy sins be forgiven thee. And, behold, certain of the scribes said within themselves, This man blasphemeth. And Jesus knowing their thoughts said, Wherefore think ye evil in your hearts? For whether is easier, to say, Thy sins be forgiven thee; or to say, Arise, and walk? But that ye may know that the Son of man hath power on earth to forgive sins, (then saith he to the sick of the palsy,) Arise, take up thy bed, and go unto thine house. And he arose, and departed to his house.*

    This passage deals with forgiveness of sin and healing. A man was brought to Jesus sick with palsy. Jesus forgave the man before He did anything else. The religious leaders became angry and muttered that Jesus had no right to forgive since He was just a man. They did not recognize he was God. Jesus, to prove he was God and had the power to forgive; He healed the man, who got up and

CHAPTER ELEVEN: FORGIVENESS

walked.

Matthew 18:21, 22: *Then came Peter to him, and said, Lord, how oft shall my brother sin against me, and I forgive him? till seven times? Jesus saith unto him, I say not unto thee, Until seven times: but, Until seventy*

Peter, trying to justify himself, asked Jesus how many times he must forgive. Jesus told him to forgive continuously, regardless of the number of offenses and how often the offenses come. We think the Lord will back us up when we want to set limits. Instead, we find out He has no limits. Just as God does not set limits on how often He will forgive us before He lowers the boom, so we can't set limits on people either.

Matthew 18:23-35: *Therefore is the kingdom of heaven likened unto a certain king, which would take account of his servants. And when he had begun to reckon, one was brought unto him, which owed him ten thousand talents. But forasmuch as he had not to pay, his lord commanded him to be sold, and his wife, and children, and all that he had, and payment to be made. The servant therefore fell down, and worshipped him, saying, Lord, have patience with me, and I will pay thee all.*

SIMPLY NEW: WALK OF THE BELIEVER

Then the lord of that servant was moved with compassion, and loosed him, and forgave him the debt. But the same servant went out, and found one of his fellowservants, which owed him an hundred pence: and he laid hands on him, and took him by the throat, saying, Pay me that thou owest. And his fellowservant fell down at his feet, and besought him, saying, Have patience with me, and I will pay thee all. And he would not: but went and cast him into prison, till he should pay the debt. So when his fellowservants saw what was done, they were very sorry, and came and told unto their lord all that was done. Then his lord, after that he had called him, said unto him, O thou wicked servant, I forgave thee all that debt, because thou desiredst me: Shouldest not thou also have had compassion on thy fellowservant, even as I had pity on thee? And his lord was wroth, and delivered him to the tormentors, till he should pay all that was due unto him. So likewise shall my heavenly Father do also unto you, if ye from your hearts forgive not every one his brother their trespasses.

    Jesus tells us the story of forgiveness. In the story, a servant was forgiven a great debt, but refused to forgive a small debt, thus resulting in great punishment. The message is this: God forgave us a great debt, we are required to forgive one another. If we don't, dire consequences come and we suffer. Too many of us want God's forgiveness, but we

CHAPTER ELEVEN: FORGIVENESS

don't want to forgive one another. We think these are two separate events. Jesus made it clear these two events are linked together. We can't have one without the other.

Mark 2:1-12: *And again he entered into Capernaum after some days; and it was noised that he was in the house. And straightway many were gathered together, insomuch that there was no room to receive them, no, not so much as about the door: and he preached the word unto them. And they come unto him, bringing one sick of the palsy, which was borne of four. And when they could not come nigh unto him for the press, they uncovered the roof where he was: and when they had broken it up, they let down the bed wherein the sick of the palsy lay. When Jesus saw their faith, he said unto the sick of the palsy, Son, thy sins be forgiven thee. But there was certain of the scribes sitting there, and reasoning in their hearts, Why doth this man thus speak blasphemies? who can forgive sins but God only? And immediately when Jesus perceived in his spirit that they so reasoned within themselves, he said unto them, Why reason ye these things in your hearts? Whether is it easier to say to the sick of the palsy, Thy sins be forgiven thee; or to say, Arise, and take up thy bed, and walk? But that ye may know that the Son of man hath power on earth to forgive sins, (he saith to the sick of the palsy,) say unto thee, Arise, and* *take up thy bed, and go thy way into thine house. And immediately he arose, took up the bed, and went forth before them all; insomuch that they were all amazed, and glorified God, saying, We never saw it on this fashion.*

    Jesus healed the man sick of the palsy. Before He healed him, Jesus told the man he was forgiven. The religious leaders had a fit. They recognized that Jesus was calling Himself God by forgiving the man. They considered Him as a mere man with no real power. Jesus proved who He said He was by healing the man. Before He did, He asked which was easier. They refused to answer.

    We have the power to forgive one another. We need to realize as we let go of one another's offenses, we will be healed. We may not be God, who does the ultimate forgiveness, but we can imitate Him with one another.

Mark 11:22-26: *And Jesus answering saith unto them, Have faith in God. For verily I say unto you, That whosoever shall say unto this mountain, Be thou removed, and be thou cast into the sea; and shall not doubt in his heart, but shall believe that those things which he saith shall come to pass; he shall have whatsoever he saith. Therefore I say unto you, What things soever ye desire, when ye pray,*

CHAPTER ELEVEN: FORGIVENESS

believe that ye receive them, and ye shall have them. And when ye stand praying, forgive, if ye have ought against any: that your Father also which is in heaven may forgive you your trespasses. But if ye do not forgive, neither will your Father which is in heaven forgive your trespasses.

We all love the first verses about speaking and believing. Those are great promises. Unfortunately, we ignore the last two. We want our cake and eat it too. We can't have God's faith for the one without the other. It takes as much faith, if not more, to forgive those who hurt us. We are just as required to forgive as when we are to speak to the mountain or believe in our hearts. In fact, the last two verses tell us what we are to believe for. Forgiveness can be very tough. The pain can be very deep. The hurt can run so deep, it's like we're in a well. We need God's faith to deal with the pain and hurt. We have two options. We can either forgive, or we can refuse. If we choose to forgive, we will have the peace of knowing we are forgiven. If we refuse, we will live in torment. The choice is up to us.

Luke 6:37, 38: *Judge not, and ye shall not be judged: condemn not, and ye shall not be condemned: forgive, and ye shall be forgiven:*

SIMPLY NEW: WALK OF THE BELIEVER

Give, and it shall be given unto you; good measure, pressed down, and shaken together, and running over, shall men give into your bosom. For with the same measure that ye mete withal it shall be measured to you again.

We are given some clear instructions. We are told not to condemn or judge. We are to forgive. While the next verse is used for money, it really refers back to the thought in the previous verse. The more we give out of these three, the more we will receive back in abundance—far greater than what we gave out. Again, we want to claim a promise without looking at the context. We must look at the whole text, not just our pet one. The next few verses go on to say we can't help others until we help ourselves. We have to ask the Lord to help us change what is in our lives through forgiveness of ourselves and removal of personal faults. We show who we are by how we behave when no one is looking. It is out of our hearts we show who we really are. This points back to the first verses which tell us how to walk out what is in our hearts. If we want good treasure, we must put in good things like forgiveness.

Luke 7:36-50: *And one of the Pharisees desired him that he would eat with him. And he went into the Pharisee's house, and sat*

CHAPTER ELEVEN: FORGIVENESS

down to meat. And, behold, a woman in the city, which was a sinner, when she knew that Jesus sat at meat in the Pharisee's house, brought an alabaster box of ointment, And stood at his feet behind him weeping, and began to wash his feet with tears, and did wipe them with the hairs of her head, and kissed his feet, and anointed them with the ointment. Now when the Pharisee which had bidden him saw it, he spake within himself, saying, This man, if he were a prophet, would have known who and what manner of woman this is that toucheth him: for she is a sinner. And Jesus answering said unto him, Simon, I have somewhat to say unto thee. And he saith, Master, say on. There was a certain creditor which had two debtors: the one owed five hundred pence, and the other fifty. And when they had nothing to pay, he frankly forgave them both. Tell me therefore, which of them will love him most? Simon answered and said, I suppose that he, to whom he forgave most. And he said unto him, Thou hast rightly judged. And he turned to the woman, and said unto Simon, Seest thou this woman? I entered into thine house, thou gavest me no water for my feet: but she hath washed my feet with tears, and wiped them with the hairs of her head. Thou gavest me no kiss: but this woman since the time I came in hath not ceased to kiss my feet. My head with oil thou didst not anoint: but this woman hath anointed my feet with ointment. Wherefore I say unto thee, Her sins, which are many, are forgiven; for she loved much: but to whom little is forgiven, the same loveth little. And he said unto her, Thy sins are forgiven. And they that sat at meat with him began to say within themselves, Who is this that forgiveth sins also? And he said to the woman, Thy faith hath saved thee; go in peace.

    We see the story of the Pharisee, the woman, and Jesus. The Pharisee invited Jesus over to dinner, but did not perform the basic duties of a host. A woman, who was a sinner, came in and washed Jesus' feet as she anointed them with ointment. The Pharisee, instead of being ashamed of his failure, criticized Jesus for not rebuking the woman. In His response, Jesus made it clear He loved both of them and forgave them. How they responded showed how much love and forgiveness they received.

    The amount of love and forgiveness we receive from the Lord, Jesus depends on how much we extend to one another. The more we extend, the more we receive. The less we extend, the less we receive. The choice is up to us. Let us extend more love and forgiveness to one another.

Luke 17:1-4: *Then said he unto the disciples, It is impossible but that offences will come: but woe unto him, through whom they come!*

CHAPTER ELEVEN: FORGIVENESS

It were better for him that a millstone were hanged about his neck, and he cast into the sea, than that he should offend one of these little ones. Take heed to yourselves: If thy brother trespass against thee, rebuke him; and if he repent, forgive him. And if he trespass against thee seven times in a day, and seven times in a day turn again to thee, saying, I repent; thou shalt forgive him.

We know offenses are going to come. People will say things or do things to hurt us. The people who hurt us will suffer consequences. While they do, if we will not forgive, we will suffer consequences as well. When a fellow believer hurts us, we are to rebuke them. We must let them know they hurt us. If they repent, we are to forgive them no matter what! We are told to not put limits on forgiveness. Matthew 18:21, 22 is an example of limitless forgiveness. The point is that we need to be like Him in every way.

<u>Acts 8:22:</u> *Repent therefore of this thy wickedness, and pray God, if perhaps the thought of thine heart may be forgiven thee.*

Peter tells Simon to repent because he tried to buy the Holy Spirit and power. It does not say if he repented or not. We need to be careful to keep our hearts right so that when we seek God, we will stay forgiven.

Ephesians 4:32: *And be ye kind one to another, tenderhearted, forgiving one another, even as God for Christ's sake hath forgiven you.*

Paul reiterates what Jesus said. We are to forgive one another. Part of forgiveness is to be kind and tenderhearted. We are to imitate Jesus because of what He had done for us. As we walk out forgiveness, we find it easier to do what Jesus asks us to do. Being kind and tenderhearted helps us stay clear from offence.

Forgiveness Between us and God.

Colossians 2:13-15: *And you, being dead in your sins and the uncircumcision of your flesh, hath he quickened together with him, having forgiven you all trespasses; Blotting out the handwriting of ordinances that was against us, which was contrary to us, and took it out of the way, nailing it to his cross; And having spoiled principalities and powers, he made a shew of them openly, triumphing over them in it.*

While we were dead in our sins, Jesus

CHAPTER ELEVEN: FORGIVENESS

forgave us. He wiped out the ordinance against us. He spoiled everything that hinders us from serving Him. All this was done at the cross when Jesus died for us. He triumphed over everything that comes against us. We have no reason to fear what may come against us. When we recognize and remember that we are forgiven—we can hold up our heads in joy—knowing we are free.

1 John 1:5-10: *This then is the message which we have heard of him, and declare unto you, that God is light, and in him is no darkness at all. If we say that we have fellowship with him, and walk in darkness, we lie, and do not the truth: if we walk in the light, as he is in the light, we have fellowship one with another, and the blood of Jesus Christ his Son cleanseth us from all sin. If we say that we have no sin, we deceive ourselves, and the truth is not in us. If we confess our sins, he is faithful and just to forgive us our sins, and to cleanse us from all unrighteousness. If we say that we have not sinned, we make him a liar, and his word is not in us.*

When we confess our sin, the Lord is quick to forgive. He cleanses us from all sin and unrighteousness. Many use this Scripture for unbelievers coming to Jesus. If we put the verse back in context, we realize this verse is directed at believers. In the previous verses, confession mentioned there is the admission we are not living what we say. If we do not admit sin, we call God a liar. His Word is not in us. Note the word "if". John is posing a series of questions. The questions ask where each person is spiritually. The final question tells us where the heart is. We need to make sure what we say matches what we do. We need to live our faith daily, not just talk about it.

Public Forgiveness.

1 Corinthians 5:1-5: *It is reported commonly that there is fornication among you, and such fornication as is not so much as named among the Gentiles, that one should have his father's wife. And ye are puffed up, and have not rather mourned, that he that hath done this deed might be taken away from among you. For I verily, as absent in body, but present in spirit, have judged already, as though I were present, concerning him that hath so done this deed, In the name of our Lord Jesus Christ, when ye are gathered together, and my spirit, with the power of our Lord Jesus Christ, To deliver such an one unto Satan for the destruction of the flesh, that the spirit may be saved in the day of the Lord Jesus.*

2 Corinthians 2:5-11: *But if any have caused*

CHAPTER ELEVEN: FORGIVENESS

grief, he hath not grieved me, but in part: that I may not overcharge you all. Sufficient to such a man is this punishment, which was inflicted of many. So that contrariwise ye ought rather to forgive him, and comfort him, lest perhaps such a one should be swallowed up with overmuch sorrow. Wherefore I beseech you that ye would confirm your love toward him. For to this end also did I write, that I might know the proof of you, whether ye be obedient in all things. To whom ye forgive any thing, I forgive also: for if I forgave any thing, to whom I forgave it, for your sakes forgave I it in the person of Christ; Lest Satan should get an advantage of us: for we are not ignorant of his devices.

    The first series of verses talk about a man in the church bragging about his sin. Paul told the Corinthian believers to turn him over to Satan so he would repent. In the second passage the man apparently repented—so Paul instructed them to forgive the man and restore him to fellowship.

    When someone in the church commits a public sin, according to Scripture, he needs to be dealt with. We need to help him to know what he is doing is wrong. Once he admits that and confesses his wrong, we are to forgive and restore him to full fellowship. Love forgives no matter what.

SIMPLY NEW: WALK OF THE BELIEVER

As we see from this study, there are various forms of forgiveness. In each of these, we see the Lord working out specific issues. As we walk out the forgiveness taught in Scripture, we will discover we have no reason to hold grudges because we have let go of the hurt.

Now, let me say this, just because we forgive does not mean we have to be around the person who hurt us. Sometimes, the best thing we can do for our own safety is to get away from the person and move on. The Lord will lead us into new relationships that are healthy for us.

Father, I come to you in repentance. I choose to forgive all who have hurt me in my life. It does not matter how bad I have been hurt. I forgive everyone. Thank you for forgiving me and keeping me safe. I pray this in Jesus name. Amen.

CHAPTER TWELVE
LOVE

Love is a very big issue. We need to walk in love to help one another. Too often, we want to pick and choose who we will love. We don't want to love those who are not like us. We need to be careful to not prejudge who we will love. It is important to make sure we seek the Lord to see how to walk in love.

There are three types of love. They are different from one another. When we understand the difference, we will be careful to walk out the type of love that is needed to minister to one another.

Eros Love

The first is Eros love. This is a love that is sensual. It is a love that keeps us happy. We say: I love my dog; I love donuts; I love the sunset; etc. These are all types of impersonal love. Eros is a love that keeps going. We see this love, in various ways, demonstrated every day.

Phileo Love

The second type of love is Phileo love. This is brotherly love. A good example of this type of love is Jonathan and David. They loved each other dearly. They exchanged items to make themselves brothers. When Jonathan told David of his father's plan to kill him, David promised to take care of his descendants. David later took care of his son. This type of love involves family and close friends. It demands that if you please me I will love you. It is not necessarily permanent but depends on people's feelings.

Agape Love

The third type of love is Agape love. It is a godly love. It is not based on what others may do for us but it is based on God. We know God loved us enough to send His Son

CHAPTER TWELVE: LOVE

to die for us. We must be willing to lay down our lives for one another to demonstrate this type of love. It is necessary to see how the Lord wants us to live.

In this chapter, I want to demonstrate how the Bible defines love through this study.

Leviticus 19:18: *Thou shalt not avenge, nor bear any grudge against the children of thy people, but thou shalt love thy neighbour as thyself: I am the Lord*

Romans 12:19: *Dearly beloved, avenge not yourselves, but rather give place unto wrath: for it is written, Vengeance is mine; I will repay, saith the Lord.*

Deuteronomy 32:35: *To me belongeth vengeance and recompence; their foot shall slide in due time: for the day of their calamity is at hand, and the things that shall come upon them make haste.*

Mark 12:31: *And the second is like, namely this, Thou shalt love thy neighbour as thyself. There is none other commandment greater than these.*

Luke 10:30—37: *And Jesus answering said, A certain man went down from Jerusalem to Jericho, and fell among thieves, which stripped him of his raiment, and wounded him, and departed, leaving him half dead. And by chance there came down a certain priest* *that way: and when he saw him, he passed by on the other side. And likewise a Levite, when he was at the place, came and looked on him, and passed by on the other side. But a certain Samaritan, as he journeyed, came where he was: and when he saw him, he had compassion on him, And went to him, and bound up his wounds, pouring in oil and wine, and set him on his own beast, and brought him to an inn, and took care of him. And on the morrow when he departed, he took out two pence, and gave them to the host, and said unto him, Take care of him; and whatsoever thou spendest more, when I come again, I will repay thee. Which now of these three, thinkest thou, was neighbour unto him that fell among the thieves? And he said, He that shewed mercy on him. Then said Jesus unto him, Go, and do thou likewise.*

    We are told to refuse to get back at fellow believers. Rather, we are to love them. We are told who has the right to seek vengeance. The Lord is the only One who can. We are told the Lord will seek vengeance by allowing the wicked to fall into trouble. Jesus told His detractors to love one another. We are to be concerned about one another to the point of ministering to them. The story of the Good Samaritan who cared for his enemy and did all he could to minister to him is a perfect example of love. Loving others includes those we don't like or

CHAPTER TWELVE: LOVE

consider our enemies. As we do, God will bless us.

Deuteronomy 6:5: *And thou shalt love the Lord thy God with all thine heart, and with all thy soul, and with all thy might.*

Matthew 22:37: *Jesus saith unto him, Thou shalt love the Lord thy God with all thy heart, and with all thy soul, and with all thy mind.*

We are commanded to love God totally with all we have. Jesus confirms this passage. He calls it the greatest commandment. This command supersedes all other commands. The other command tells us how to walk out this love. We need to realize loving your neighbor comes directly out of the love we have for God.

Proverbs 10:12: *Hatred stirreth up strifes: but love covereth all sins.*

1 Corinthians 13:4-7: *Charity suffereth long, and is kind; charity envieth not; charity vaunteth not itself, is not puffed up, Doth not behave itself unseemly, seeketh not her own, is not easily provoked, thinketh no evil; Rejoiceth not in iniquity, but rejoiceth in the truth; Beareth all things, believeth all things, hopeth all things, endureth all things.*

Hatred causes strife. It causes problems for us. Love covers sin. Love takes the time to stop judging and hurting one another. This passage tells us how love behaves. It takes time to care and see how to get through difficulties.

Ecclesiastes 3:8: *A time to love, and a time to hate; a time of war, and a time of peace.*

Luke 14:26: *If any man come to me, and hate not his father, and mother, and wife, and children, and brethren, and sisters, yea, and his own life also, he cannot be my disciple.*

Song of Solomon 2:4: *He brought me to the banqueting house, and his banner over me was love.*

There is a time when love is preeminent. There is a time when hate comes. We need to remember others are secondary to the Lord. "Hate", here, means to put in second place. There is a place for each. The Lord brings us to a place where He leads us in His home. He posts a banner above us telling us of His love. He shows everyone how to have love for us.

John 14:15: *If ye love me, keep my commandments*

CHAPTER TWELVE: LOVE

1 John 5:3: *For this is the love of God, that we keep his commandments: and his commandments are not grievous.*

As believers, we are commanded to keep the Lord's commands. This proves we love Him. The commandments are not hard or burdensome. Burdensome means heavy, grievous to be borne, causing uneasiness or fatigue; repressive. In other words, commands are able to be done in peace through the love of the Father. I am not saying it is easy, but I am saying it can be done. The Lord never gives us anything we can't handle. So it is obvious we can handle the commands.

John 15:12: *This is my commandment, that ye love one another, as I have loved you.*

John 13:34: *A new commandment I give unto you, That ye love one another; as I have loved you, that ye also love one another.*

1 John 3:11: *For this is the message that ye have heard from the beginning, that we should love one another*

One of the commands we are to obey is to love one another. We need to remember our love is based on the love of the Father.

Jesus gave us a new command. We are to love one another as He loves us. Jesus loves us with the love of the Father. We have heard this message from the beginning. Jesus taught us to love one another from the beginning of His ministry. It is obvious love is very important.

<u>Romans 12:9:</u> *Let love be without dissimulation. Abhor that which is evil; cleave to that which is good.*

<u>1 Timothy 1:5:</u> *Now the end of the commandment is charity out of a pure heart, and of a good conscience, and of faith unfeigned*

<u>Psalms 34:14:</u> *Depart from evil, and do good; seek peace, and pursue it.*

Our love must be real. It must be shown in our actions. We are to detest evil. We are to have nothing to do with it. We are to cling to all that is good. We are to hold on to the things which benefit others. This love comes because we stay pure with knowing what right and honest faith is. It must be fair and complete. We are to leave evil and do good. We are to seek peace and chase it. We are to do everything in our power to avoid and do away with anything that is harmful while searching for and chasing everything

CHAPTER TWELVE: LOVE

that blesses each other.

1 Corinthians 8:1: Now as touching things offered unto idols, we know that we all have knowledge. Knowledge puffeth up but charity edifieth.

2 Corinthians 6:14-18: Be ye not unequally yoked together with unbelievers: for what fellowship hath righteousness with unrighteousness? and what communion hath light with darkness? And what concord hath Christ with Belial? or what part hath he that believeth with an infidel? And what agreement hath the temple of God with idols? for ye are the temple of the living God; as God hath said, I will dwell in them, and walk in them; and I will be their God, and they shall be my people. Wherefore come out from among them, and be ye separate, saith the Lord, and touch not the unclean thing; and I will receive you. And will be a Father unto you, and ye shall be my sons and daughters, saith the Lord Almighty.

We are to put away everything that stands between us and God. We have knowledge of those things. We are told to not be unequally yoke to anyone who does not serve the Lord. We need to stay away from anything that is not appropriate in our lives— we have no excuse. The sad thing is, there are times when this knowledge causes pride. Love edifies or lifts us up.

1 Corinthians 13:8: *Charity never faileth: but whether there be prophecies, they shall fail; whether there be tongues, they shall cease; whether there be knowledge, it shall vanish away.*

Love never fails. It never goes away. Different gifts may pass away or, for any reason, knowledge stops. Love stays to minister to one another. In the verses before, we see how love operates. As we walk in love, we will see God move in major ways. Some denominations say these gifts have passed away with the early disciples. They claim knowledge is no longer needed because we have a complete Bible. The truth is, they still exist because knowledge still exists. As we study the Bible, the Holy Spirit guides us into all truth. Because of this, the gifts of the Spirit are still available to us. The point Paul is making is, love is far greater than any gift or knowledge. It will endure until Jesus comes to take us on into the heavenly realm.

2 Corinthians 5: 14,15: *For the love of Christ constraineth us; because we thus judge, that*

CHAPTER TWELVE: LOVE

if one died for all, then were all dead: And that he died for all, that they which live should not henceforth live unto themselves, but unto him which died for them, and rose again.

The love of God urges us to realize that, because Jesus died for us, we are dead to sin. We are not to live to ourselves but to Jesus who died for us. Jesus constrains us. This means to employ force contrary to nature and right—to compel by using force; to hold together, confine, secure, or to hold fast. In other words, we are compelled to hold fast to the love of God so we can grow in the Lord.

Galatians 5:22,23: *But the fruit of the Spirit is love, joy, peace, longsuffering, gentleness, goodness, faith, Meekness, temperance: against such there is no law.*

Romans 15:2: *Let every one of us please his neighbour for his good to edification.*

Part of the fruit of the Spirit is love. Out of love comes the rest of the fruit. Love is foremost. We are to seek to please our neighbor to build up one another. We are to aim to help one another for their benefit. Love does the seeking because it wants the best for all.

Ephesians 5:25-27: *Husbands, love your wives, even as Christ also loved the church,* *and gave himself for it; That he might sanctify and cleanse it with the washing of water by the word, That he might present it to himself a glorious church, not having spot, or wrinkle, or any such thing; but that it should be holy and without blemish.*

Husbands are commanded to love their wives. They need to see and follow the example of Jesus who gave His life for His bride out of His love. Jesus sets apart His body to cleanse it and make it holy. He wants to remove anything that is unclean or hinders the body. A similar thing is true of the husbands. They are to do everything possible to help their wives grow and remove all things that hinder them.

Titus 2:3-5: *The aged women likewise, that they be in behaviour as becometh holiness, not false accusers, not given to much wine, teachers of good things; That they may teach the young women to be sober, to love their husbands, to love their children, To be discreet, chaste, keepers at home, good, obedient to their own husbands, that the word of God be not blasphemed.*

We, older women, are to admonish or teach young women to love their husbands and children. They are to put their families first. We are to teach by example. We are

CHAPTER TWELVE: LOVE

to walk in holiness. We teach the younger women to be careful to do what is necessary to help their families grow and mature. By doing this, we are actually applying the Word of God to our lives.

1 Peter 4:8: *And above all things have fervent charity among yourselves: for charity shall cover the multitudes of sins.*

We are to be ardent, very warm, earnest, excited, animated with love for each other. God's love will cover many sins. This love makes sure help is brought to the person who needs help. Love keeps us on track. Love covers sin to the point where there is forgiveness.

1 John 3:14: *We know that we have passed from death unto life, because we love the brethren. He that loveth not his brother abideth in death.*

We can prove that we have left death and entered into life, because we love our fellow believers. If we do not love our brothers, we live in death. When we love one another, we walk in life and light. We need to make a choice which way we want to go. We have a choice between life and death. Let us choose life through love.

1 John 4:7-9: *Beloved, let us love one another: for love is of God; and every one that loveth is born of God, and knoweth God. He that loveth not knoweth not God; for God is love. this was manifested the love of God toward us, because that God sent his only begotten Son into the world, that we might live through him.*

If we do not love one another we do not really know God. God is love. When we refuse to love, we are saying God does not care. Love is the very motive of God. He cares about us. We need to take on the nature of God. We need to love one another. We want to prove we are born of God and know Him. We prove it by our love for one another. The love of God is shown by sending His Son into the world. We need to accept that love.

Revelation 2:4: *Nevertheless I have somewhat against thee, because thou hast left thy first love.*

Revelation 3:15,16: *I know thy works, that*

CHAPTER TWELVE: LOVE

thou art neither cold nor hot: I would thou wert cold or hot. So then because thou art lukewarm, and neither cold nor hot, I will spue thee out of my mouth.

We must remember our first love is Jesus. When we forget, we grow cold. We must be either hot or cold. We must stop being lukewarm. When we are lukewarm, we forsake love. We put it away. We need to be on fire walking in love. When we admit we have left our first love, we can come back to the Lord and get the healing we need. The problem is, we either don't recognize we have fallen away, or do not care. Either way, we are in trouble. Let us come back to our first love and serve the Lord.

The love described above is not an "ooey gooey" form of love based on feelings. It is an act of our will. We choose to love as the Lord gives us the ability. We have a choice, we can either obey the Lord in our walk of love or we can ignore what He says. As we choose to obey the Lord, we will see victory in our lives. We want to stop being stubborn and be on fire for the Lord as we walk out His love.

Let us choose to walk in love regardless of what we might think or want. We need to settle in our minds we will do what the Word says regardless of what the world thinks. Let us be obedient to the Lord Jesus.

SIMPLY NEW: WALK OF THE BELIEVER

CHAPTER THIRTEEN
OUR DAILY WALK PT. TWO

Now that we have looked at a number of things that are important to our walk, we will look at how to walk out our daily walk. We make a choice to do what God wants. As we seek the Lord to have Him do what He wants in our lives.

We need to remember who we are in the Lord. We are the righteousness of God in Christ. We are saved by grace in Jesus. It is through the work of Jesus, we are complete. We have nothing to fear, because Jesus takes care of us. As believers, we can do anything we want to do in Jesus, but we must be willing to do the will of God.

Romans 5:20,21: *Moreover the law entered, that the offence might abound. But where sin abounded, grace did much more abound: That as sin hath reigned unto death, even so might grace reign through righteousness unto eternal life by Jesus Christ our Lord.*

Philippians 4:13: *I can do all things through Christ which strengtheneth me.*

As we can see, we are made righteous in Jesus. We are no longer bound by sin. We have the grace of God making us righteous in Jesus. Because we are righteous, we want to do what the Lord wants in our lives. As we do what the Lord wants, He will give us strength to do it.

Spiritual Warfare

An area not covered in the above chapters is spiritual warfare. It is basically intercession for others who want to serve the Lord or need to be saved. It is part of our daily walk. Spiritual warfare stops the enemy from attacking believers.

CHAPTER THIRTEEN: OUR DAILY WALK PT. TWO

2 Corinthians 10:3-6: For though we walk in the flesh, we do not war after the flesh: (For the weapons of our warfare are not carnal, but mighty through God to the pulling down of strong holds;) Casting down imaginations, and every high thing that exalteth itself against the knowledge of God, and bringing into captivity every thought to the obedience of Christ; And having in a readiness to revenge all disobedience, when your obedience is fulfilled.

Ephesians 6:10-20: Finally, my brethren, be strong in the Lord, and in the power of his might. Put on the whole armour of God, that ye may be able to stand against the wiles of the devil. For we wrestle not against flesh and blood, but against principalities, against powers, against the rulers of the darkness of this world, against spiritual wickedness in high places. Wherefore take unto you the whole armour of God, that ye may be able to withstand in the evil day, and having done all, to stand. Stand therefore, having your loins girt about with truth, and having on the breastplate of righteousness; And your feet shod with the preparation of the gospel of peace; Above all, taking the shield of faith, wherewith ye shall be able to quench all the fiery darts of the wicked. And take the helmet of salvation, and the sword of the Spirit, which is the word of God: Praying always with all prayer and supplication in the Spirit, and watching thereunto with all perseverance *and supplication for all saints; And for me, that utterance may be given unto me, that I may open my mouth boldly, to make known the mystery of the gospel, For which I am an ambassador in bonds: that therein I may speak boldly, as I ought to speak.*

    We are to put down thoughts which keep us from serving the Lord. We are to cast down all vain imaginations. We are to take captive any thoughts that keep us from living victoriously. This is all part of spiritual warfare.

    We have been told we do not fight against flesh and blood. We are not fighting one another, though it seems like it. Rather, we are fighting the enemy and his imps. Just like the military has ranks, so does the enemy. We fight all the different ranks at one time or another. In intercession, we are stopping them from harming the ones we are praying for.

    As part of our walk, we are to put on the full armor of God. We are to make sure we are totally covered. Interestingly enough all the armor covers the front side. It does not cover the back. This tells us we are not to turn tail and run for we are not protected. Rather, we are to stand before the enemy and allow the Lord to fight our battles. We do our part by standing and praying the Scripture.

CHAPTER THIRTEEN: OUR DAILY WALK PT. TWO

We have nothing to be afraid of because the Lord is on our side.

In our daily walk we are to do what we can to stand firm in the Word and in prayer. The other things listed above are to strengthen us to walk in a manner that is pleasing to the Lord. As we fellowship with others, we learn from them and grow in our knowledge of the Lord and His Word. As we give to support the ministry, we receive blessings from the Lord. Mind you, we are not seeking the blessings; we are being obedient to the Lord.

When we choose to walk in forgiveness and love, we are imitating the Lord in our walk. We recognize we were commanded to do these things. The choice is up to us. Let us remember to walk in obedience to the Lord in these areas.

Our daily walk is very full. We have no room for anything that does not please the Lord. When we choose to disobey, we walk into the enemy's trap. We need to avoid it by staying as close to the Lord as possible.

MY WALK WITH GOD

JOURNAL SECTION

www.ingramcontent.com/pod-product-compliance
Lightning Source LLC
Chambersburg PA
CBHW071630080526
44588CB00010B/1339